TEACHING
CHILDREN
TO RIDE

A Handbook for Instructors

TEACHING CHILDREN TO RIDE

A Handbook for Instructors

JANE WALLACE

KENILWORTH PRESS

Dedication

*I would like to dedicate this book to Liz Pickard,
my mentor from an early age and the most wonderful teacher.
I count myself incredibly lucky to have been one of hundreds of
young riders taught by her in my childhood. She instilled such
confidence and enthusiasm in her pupils, and her lessons were
always tremendous fun. She has been a great source of
inspiration to me in many ways.*

First published in Great Britain 2002 by
Kenilworth Press
Addington
Buckingham
MK18 2JR

Reprinted 2003 and 2004 (twice)

British Library Cataloguing in Publication Data
A CIP record for this book is available from the British Library

ISBN 1-872119-43-3

Illustrations by **Dianne Breeze** (except that on page 3, which is by Carole Vincer)
Diagrams by **Michael J. Stevens**
Cover illustrations by **Carole Vincer, Dianne Breeze and Michael J. Stevens**

Typesetting and layout by Kenilworth Press

Printed and bound in Great Britain by Bell & Bain

CONTENTS

FOREWORD by Lucinda Green, MBE

This book is a MUST for anyone wanting their children to grow into riders that are good enough to enjoy and succeed in any area of riding they might choose.

As my experience lies in teaching grown-ups, I rather wondered if I was the right person to write a foreword to this book. As I read it, repeatedly I found reference to the logic that has developed my own teaching. The need for everything to be FUN, the importance of helping someone to become dextrous with their riding whilst, critically, never to frighten or undermine them.

This is a truly wonderful book, full of inspirational, challenging ideas to achieve the above. The best steeplechase jockeys in the world, and hence, I believe, the greatest horsemen, are reared in Ireland. The jockeys have developed their superior balance and feel for a horse, principally through having little enough money and just 'getting on with it'. Many went hunting without the saddles they could not afford.

Recreating this in the politically correct, increasingly moneyed world in which we now have to bring up our children, is almost impossible. Jane Wallace, in this collection of wisdom and fun, has come very close to the equivalent but in a controlled and safe environment.

The book concludes at Chapter 13. There still remains no substitute for Chapter 14 – Hunting. To maintain that freedom of choice is a fight we must never relinquish – if we care where our children are going and how they are going there.

Lucinda Green

ACKNOWLEDGEMENTS

I would like to thank Liz Pickard, Maureen Chamberlain, Gill and Katherine Painter, Margaret Wilkin, Emma Staines, Sarah Charles and Peter Hales for their time and inspiration in contributing to this book.

I am grateful to the following children who acted as models for the illustrations: Giles and Rosie Newton, Eleanor and Bea Saunders-Watson, and Tom and Charlie Wallace; and Nicky Herbert for her help in setting up the photographs (on which many of the illustrations are based), taken during a lesson she gave to my son Tom.

I would also like to thank Dianne Breeze for her superb drawings; and Michael Stevens for his excellent diagrams.

JANE WALLACE

INTRODUCTION

Now that I have retired from competitive riding, I devote myself to teaching various standards and age groups. As the mother of two sons aged six and eight, both of whom are learning to ride, I can vouch for the fact that teaching one's own children proves to be by far the most difficult!

A combination of the vast differences in the teaching abilities in those entrusted to educating young riders and the sparsity of suitable books on this subject has prompted me to put pen to paper again. I hope that this book, with its collection of practical and fun ideas for lessons and riding activities, will be a source of inspiration to established teachers as well as to those less experienced.

Teaching the youngest age brackct of four- to nine-year-olds is possibly the most taxing. It is hard work. It requires patience, understanding, firmness and huge enthusiasm from the teacher. Although it is not vital, many of the best teachers of this age group are parents themselves (ideally not of the actual children being taught) who have learnt over the years the best way of cajoling and enthusing children to try new things.

Once a child is in control of his pony, understands school movements, knows right from left, and has the basic knowledge of why he is being asked to perform various

movements, he becomes much less difficult to teach. No instructor would disagree that the older age groups are, on the whole, much easier to manage. Young children have a short attention span and the teacher has to be quick to realise when that concentration is coming to a close. A change to something different is crucial before the children become bored, tired or distracted. Holding the attention of anyone is difficult; holding the attention of small children is definitely an art or knack but it is something which can be learnt from trial and error and, of course, experience. There is no substitute for experience in any walk of life and to be a good teacher rcquires it in large doses. An instructor needs to gain a sixth sense, that special ability to assess a situation, anticipate a potentially hazardous one and yet enable him to hold the interest and enthusiasm of the children in the ride. To acquire this requires practice. However, practice does not necessarily make perfect. Practice makes permanent, so if you practise the wrong thing, you will not improve (ask any golfer, for example!) so you must know what you are trying to do before you can achieve results. This is where this book will be of value.

In writing this book I have interviewed a number of experienced, talented teachers who excel in teaching young children. I clearly recall my early riding lessons with Liz Pickard at Cherry Hinton Riding School. Miss P, as she was fondly called, was an inspiration to us all. All age groups idolised her. We all had a very healthy respect for her too, but she had that true magic of making children (and grown-ups too) want to please her and gain her praise. She had a unique way with children, and could understand a child's mind and way of thinking. She was able to enthuse and encourage, and she gave enormous confidence to those she taught. I was lucky to be included in her long list of pupils. Needless to say, Miss P was the first person I thought of when the idea of this book came to me. If I could glean ideas and hints from her, plus other people with that special talent, I could produce a useful and informative manual, which would help us all, myself included.

As well as talking to Liz Pickard, I also spoke to Margaret Wilkin, Gill and Katherine Painter,

Sarah Charles, Emma Staines, Peter Haines and Maureen Chamberlain – all gifted instructors who manage to enthuse and inspire.

It was a fascinating insight talking to these people and they generously supplied me with all sorts of ideas. In passing on their thoughts, and my own, I hope that this book will become an invaluable source of reference for all those interested in improving their methods of instruction. Children are so vulnerable and can easily be frightened or put off by lack of good teaching. Fear, discomfort or boredom can soon make even the keenest child view riding with reluctance and alarm. Enthusiasm must be maintained at all times.

At the end of a lesson, children should always be asking for more! 'Can I come again next time, please?' is what every instructor loves to hear.

1 PLANNING A LESSON

Before any lesson, whether it be for adults or children, a certain amount of preparation is necessary. In the case of a group lesson for children, this forward planning can make the difference between a successful lesson and a mediocre one.

FACTS TO ASCERTAIN

How old are the children? Until you know the age of the riders you cannot plan your lesson.

What standard are they? It is important to know what the children and ponies are capable of doing. For example: will they need leading? Are there any notoriously difficult ponies, or particularly nervous children?

How many will there be? Teaching young children in a group is an advantage. Children love to be amongst their peers and it gives them enthusiasm and courage. However, a big group lesson requires careful planning to avoid boredom among those not actually involved 'in the action'. The ideal size of group would be between four and six, although it does depend of the standard of riders. When teaching children you need to have 'eyes in the back of your head' and any more than six means that

you could find yourself struggling to keep an eye on everyone.

Where is the lesson to be held? An enclosed area with a soft surface is preferable for safety reasons. Trying to control small children on ponies in an unrestricted area should be avoided.

What is the weather likely to be? Inclement or hot conditions can make teaching difficult. It is important to have contingency plans to cope with adverse weather. Be aware of the effect a wind can have on any pony and especially a 'sharp' one. Find out where shelter or shade is likely to be and plan to make use of it. Small children get cold very easily, so plan some vigorous activity to avoid frozen toes and fingers. There is nothing more likely to discourage a child from riding than getting frozen stiff.

How long is the session? You cannot plan a lesson unless you know its duration. However

> *"Be pleasant and constructive, and have a well-prepared lesson."* **Peter Hales**

11

SUITABLE PROPS

A selection of the following can be kept in a portable container which fits easily in your car to be taken with you whenever you are teaching.

String – twine is invaluable. It can improvise as grass reins if required, be used to tie up the letter-boxes (see below) and generally come in handy.

Spare stirrup leathers – to use as neck-straps. All ponies should have a neck-strap.

Thick elastic bands – these can be used as rein stops to help a child maintain a suitable length of rein. Can also improvise as lost keepers or runners on bridles or neck-straps.

A **hole-punch** can be useful.

Cones, bollards or plastic buckets or containers with letters on them – plastic markers are far safer than something heavy and solid, which could hurt a child in the event of a fall.

Flags on canes – to be put into bollards or cones.

Buckets (plastic) – for games.

Balls or bean-bags – suitable for throwing into buckets.

Potatoes and spoons.

Letter-boxes – made from cardboard boxes, painted red with a slot for posting letters – and letters for posting.

Batons or hankies – for passing hand to hand.

Poles – usually these are provided but always check.

Seasonal items – such as tinsel at Christmas.

Music player and music – an invaluable addition to lessons but check that it would be an appropriate situation.

Milk-crate or similar portable block – to practise mounting

Items of grooming kit, a shoe, farriers' tools, first aid equipment, tack, boots, bits, and anything for the children to touch and feel – for quiet moments of stable management.

Sticky labels with the points of the horse written on them – a fun way of learning with an amenable pony.

Leaves – these can be used for all kinds of activities and are normally available wherever the lesson may be.

Large sheets of paper – for drawing on, and pens/pencils.

Overreach boots – you can use these as markers, upside-down, to go round in corners, pretending they are rabbit holes.

long it is to be, it will be necessary to change the activities regularly to break up the lesson and avoid the children losing concentration.

Is this a one-off lesson or part of a series? If you know the children and they know you and each other, you would not start the lesson in the same way as if everyone were new to each other. This also affects the lesson content.

Are there any props available? Some schools are well equipped; others have nothing at all. You need to know what you should provide but until you know the answers to some of the earlier questions, e.g. the age of the children and the length of the lesson, you will not know what sort of props you might require. It is worth collecting items that you can use to play games with the children.

Refreshments – are any provided? Should you provide some, and if so are there any children with allergies or who cannot eat certain things? Drink – is juice provided? Children respond much better if their blood sugar is kept up. Find out when the refreshments will arrive (if at all) so you can plan your lesson to fit in with the break.

Is there a policy regarding jackets or jumpers for the children to wear? I would

"Teaching is all about liking children and encouraging them. No bunch of children is ever the same." **Margaret Wilkin**

always prefer children to ride in jumpers. Jackets can make them rigid and less relaxed. Thick coats make it difficult to see whether a child is sitting up or slouching.

For additional safety considerations regarding dress, whips, etc. see Rider check, page 36. See also notes about riding hats on page 18.

THE LESSON PLAN

Once you have the answers to all the above questions you can start to make a plan for the lesson. Obviously situations may change – the weather may vary for example, or the number of pupils may be different – but on the whole you will have a general idea of what to expect.

Bearing in mind that learning must be fun, it is important to structure the lesson so that the 'serious' parts are interspersed with some fun action. There is no doubt that boys, on the whole, have a totally different attitude to riding from girls. This must be remembered when teaching little boys. Boys soon get fed up with riding in the school unless it is made fun. They are rarely interested in the 'finesse' side of riding or in stable management but merely want to climb on their ponies and go! Canter, gallop and jump (once they are capable of so doing) is all they want to do. So, to maintain interest, it is vital that lessons are exciting and interesting with plenty of activity to avoid boys becoming bored and distracted. A group of boys can be great fun to teach, but you have to be well prepared with plenty of different ideas, activities and games to play.

EXAMPLE LESSON PLAN

1. Introductions (greet your riders and helpers).

2. Tack and rider check (**always** do a tack check and look at what your riders are wearing too).

3. Riding action. (This will be one of the most receptive times because the children will not be tired. After ten or fifteen minutes it will be time to change to something different and give the children a rest.)

4. Mounted exercises.

5. Refreshments. (Always popular!)

6. Riding action. (The children should again be in receptive mood with recharged batteries. Spend ten or fifteen minutes then again change to something different.)

7. 'Jumping', i.e. riding over poles, or mounted games.

8. Wind-down period (so you do not hand back an over-excited ride).

When you know the duration of the session you can decide how many different parts to the lesson will be needed. This means that you divide the lesson up into sections. Long sessions of teaching are counterproductive because children get tired, lose concentration and may then view lessons with a lack of enthusiasm. After an hour on a pony, a child will be *more* than ready to get off, so make sure you plan to allow for the length of the lesson. Never over-do things. Always stop while the children are keen.

Decide carefully which are the appropriate activities for your particular ride on that day in those circumstances. Better to be safe than sorry. There is a thin line between safety and everything ending in tears.

Plan to arrive at the venue in good time so you

> "*Teaching children is very hard work. You must have authority and you need to understand children and ponies.*"
> **Gill Painter**

can get organised. You can put your props in position, mark out your arena if necessary, and have time to find out more about the members of your ride. You should be given a list with the names of the children, and preferably the ponies too, and you should try to find out who everyone is before you begin. (It gives the pupils a good feeling if you appear to know who they are and what their pony is called without being told!)

Make sure you are neatly turned out. Children are quick to assess people and will soon decide

> *"Be happy! If you are happy, you have fun. Our children must go home having had fun as well as being educated."* **Emma Staines**

if this instructor is one to respect or trifle with. A well-turned out, bright, enthusiastic person, who is well organised and in charge of the situation, will gain the children's attention from the outset.

2 BEFORE YOU BEGIN

SAFETY FIRST

Now more than ever, with the threat of litigation hanging over everyone who teaches, it is vital to be aware of safety. Without being paranoid, it is a case of being sensible, thoughtful and alert for potentially hazardous situations. Accidents will always happen but so many can be averted by vigilance.

- The area for teaching must have a suitable surface. A hard, rutted field is dangerous because the ponies are liable to trip. If a child falls off onto hard ground it could hurt considerably more than landing on a soft, flat surface.

- The teaching area should not be too big (20 x 40 metres is maximum) and must be enclosed with adequate fencing and a gate that fastens securely.

NOTE: Always have a phone to hand when you are teaching, and also when hacking out, in case of emergencies. (Mobile phones are invaluable, but make sure yours is turned off unless required!)

- You should always carry out a tack and rider check before the lesson starts.

- Always line the ride up in an orderly fashion to avoid kicking. Stress the importance of keeping one pony's distance when in a ride, and indeed at all times when behind another pony. An unruly ride is a dangerous ride. Discipline is important at all times.

"Being a good teacher is firstly personality and secondly knowledge and experience. You must have your finger on the pulse I cannot bear to see raucous rides. I want them to learn something. But it has got to be fun alongside teaching. Be nice!"
Liz Pickard

RIDING HATS

The safety of riding hats is under constant review and new, improved designs are produced every few years. Remind parents to check that their child's hat conforms to the latest safety requirements.

If a child has a heavy fall, or the hat is dropped

Correctly fitted crash cap with silk. Hair neatly tucked away.

Hat too big and perched on the back of the head giving no protection to the forehead.

onto a hard surface, the effectiveness of the hat will be impaired. Hats are expensive, but not more than a child's safety so they should always be replaced if damaged. (Unless the damage is extensive, it will not be visible to the naked eye, so ask the advice of a reputable saddler if in doubt whether a new one is necessary or not.)

Chinstrap too loose, allowing hat to slip back and even become dislodged altogether.

If you have any doubts about the fitting of any hat, recommend that the parents go to a good saddler's shop to check the size and fitting.

DISCIPLINE

Discipline must be maintained for:

1. Safety – undisciplined riding can easily lead to accidents.

2. Progress – children cannot learn if they are inattentive or ignore instructions.

3. Manners – good manners are important in all walks of life.

4. Concentration requires discipline.

5. An undisciplined child will disrupt a lesson and prevent other children from getting the benefit of your instruction.

6. Remember – a child without discipline is like a ship without a rudder.

Some children will take advantage of a young instructor and think they can get away with being naughty and rude. You need to make it clear from the outset that you are in charge by being firm and positive and that you expect to be obeyed. If you allow the lesson to become dull, boring or beyond the capabilities of your pupils, you will be asking for trouble. This is why it is so important to pre-plan your lesson and be ready to move onto something different if it is blatantly clear that the present activity is inappropriate.

If children are kept amused and interested they are far less likely to cause trouble. However, if any child deliberately misbehaves, it is within your right to correct him. You need ingenuity to decide how best to do this. Either prevent the child from doing an activity you know he enjoys, or if the child is particularly exuberant, you could always make him run round the school to get rid of excess energy.

If a child is being persistently bad and disrupting the lesson, yet despite warnings that you will send him from the lesson, he continues to misbehave, you should send him out, explaining calmly to the parents why it was necessary. Point out that discipline is essential for the safety of the child. If you are being paid to teach the child, you must be prepared to refund the money.

AWARENESS AND ANTICIPATION

It is imperative that you are constantly on your guard and always on the look-out for possible problems. Children are not aware of potentially dangerous situations until they become reasonably mature, so you must be alert to children's lack of thought and foresight. You need to constantly remind children to pull up in time so they do not get too close to the pony in front, to keep ponies away from each other so that they cannot touch noses (in case they squeal and kick out), to keep to the centre of gateways so they can't catch their toe or knee on the gatepost, to duck when riding under branches, to give fence wings or other ponies enough room so they do not bump into them. You need to think for the children. Do not expect them to think for themselves, because they will not!

THE COMFORT FACTOR

Be observant for any child looking as if he is uncomfortable in any way. Children are often reluctant to say if anything hurts and much too shy, on the whole, to say they need to 'spend a

> **NOTE**: Many children stick out their tongue when they are trying hard or concentrating. This must be corrected and stopped because a child could severely bite his tongue, causing a nasty injury if the pony stumbled.

penny'. Watch out for any surreptitious wriggling or tugging of jodhpurs. There may be a wrinkle in an awkward place or the child could be desperate to go to the loo. (With little ones, it is a good idea to check whether anyone needs to go before the lesson begins.) It is quite common for a child to get a 'stitch' when trotting, so keep a constant look out for signs of distress that may indicate something is amiss.

FALLING OFF

Despite taking all possible precautions, it is inevitable that a child will fall off at some stage. To minimise the risk, remember the following points:

1. Avoid compromising situations by anticipating possible problems.

2. Make sure all equipment is safe.

3. When jumping, make sure the jumps are small and easy. Never use anything spooky to build a fence because this can cause a pony to take a huge leap, so unbalancing the rider.

4. Introduce new work gradually and only when the child is ready to do it.

5. When jumping, minimise the risk of injury by constructing and siting the fence sensibly.

6. If in doubt, don't. There is always another day.

If, despite all reasonable care, a child does fall off, try not to make a big issue of it. Assess the situation as quickly as possible. By the nature of the fall, you should know whether the child is likely to have suffered a major injury. Do not be overly hearty, but make minimum fuss. If the child gets up immediately and is obviously not hurt in the least, you can be quite jolly and say something like, 'Oh dear, now what were you doing?' or 'Did you mean to dismount then?' and pop the child back onto the pony as quickly as possible, checking 'OK? No bruises?'

If a rider lands heavily and is winded or shocked, take your time and comfort the child, assessing if there is any injury, without fussing unduly. Provided that the child is uninjured, he should be put back on his pony as soon as possible.

Although serious injuries at this stage rarely occur, you must be prepared for any eventuality.

It is imperative that all instructors have attended an equine-related injuries first aid course and hold an up-to-date certificate.

If a child does fall awkwardly, which suggests he may have suffered injury, it is vital that you do not panic, but act in accordance with your knowledge from your first-aid course.

Children may react differently from adults when they fall off. Silence on landing may be the result of being winded and frightened, and loud crying may soon follow (always a relief to hear). Check carefully for any sign of injury, and examine the child's hat for signs of damage. (If a child is wearing glasses, make sure they are undamaged, or, if they have fallen off, that they are not trodden on.)

Try to calm the child after he has fallen off by asking questions and making sure he realises that he fell off, and that it was not his pony's fault. You could explain that his pony is really upset that his rider fell off; that his rider is crying; that his rider doesn't want to get back on again, etc. and that the pony needs comforting by the child getting back on again.

If the pony was misbehaving, you can try the line of 'We mustn't let him get away with it.' However, if you think that a repeat performance is at all likely then you must take action to avoid it. Either ride the pony yourself or lunge it, and then have a leader for the child when he gets back on. It is crucial that the child recovers confidence from the tumble as quickly as possible, so it may be necessary to substitute another pony or make the work easier so that the lesson finishes on a good note.

Each Pony Club branch, and indeed any official establishment, keeps a report of every accident, where any fall is recorded with the time, date, venue and details of the fall and any injuries which is then signed by the instructor and preferably a witness too. On other occasions, it is advisable to keep your own written evidence of any fall where a child is injured for your own protection in case of possible future litigation.

There is an example of an Accident Report Form

in a useful booklet published by the British Horse Society for the British Equestrian Federation entitled *Duty of Care, Guidelines for the Horse Industry,* incorporating child protection guidelines. This is an invaluable source of information covering a number of important subjects, including risk assessment. I strongly recommend that anyone teaching children obtains a copy of this booklet and reads it carefully. If you are teaching for a recognised organisation, it will have done its own risk assessment, but it is your responsibility to be observant and diligent when teaching and dealing with young children.

Although litigation cases are uncommon, make sure that your insurance is valid and up to date. You are covered by the Pony Club's insurance policy when you teach at an official Pony Club activity, but check other situations.

DEALING WITH 'DIFFICULT' PONIES

If you think that a pony is so unsuitable for the child riding it as to present a hazard to that child or the rest of the ride, it is your duty to say so. It may be that the pony is over-fresh and would benefit from being lunged for a time to get rid of over-exuberance. This may not be practical at that particular moment –say, if you are about to take a lesson with a number of other children – but you could suggest it for another time.

Ensure that any pony which is being difficult is led by someone experienced who knows how to handle the situation. If the pony is excitable, it is imperative that the leader does not try to suppress the exuberance too strongly because ponies tend to rear if the energy is not allowed to move forwards.

If the child is frightened, and the pony is still being naughty and will scare the child even more, then let the child dismount and help you take the lesson. There are always little jobs that a child can do to involve him in the lesson, even if on foot. There are, for example, competitions to judge, poles to move, props to find, refreshments to give out. The child will then be much happier, and once a more suitable pony is available (and this is vital for restoring confidence), the child will be much more willing to join in next time.

Never frighten a child riding a pony. He or she will never forget the bad experience.

Even if the pony is behaving appallingly, try to be positive about what you say and do not overly criticise it. You can say that he is being very naughty and needs some hard work, but do not call him every name under the sun (even if it deserves it!). This would make the child view ponies in a bad light, and it is important that children do actually love their ponies and not start to dislike them. If you put into a child's head the idea that his pony is a brute, then he may well take that to heart.

RUNNERS/LEADERS

It must be stressed that the leader is in charge of the child and pony he is leading.

1. Runners or leaders need to be able to run fast

Leader running correctly beside rider, watching carefully for any loss of balance or lack of security.

Leader correctly holding child's lower leg but, rather than watching the child, making sure that she does not trip over the pole herself.

enough (and long enough!) to allow the pony to trot as necessary.

2. They must be able to hold on to the child's leg if need be, and this is all the more important when jumping.

3. The runner must be a responsible person who is aware of the child and pony at all times. They must be experienced enough to anticipate an 'anxious moment' and prevent it turning into an accident.

4. Young children are not suitable as leaders, neither are non-horsey parents.

5. A child tends to try harder for someone who is not a parent. An insecure child might insist on having a parent, which is fine. For a young instructor the presence of a parent can be intimidating, but you must remember that *you* are teaching the child and that *you* are in charge of the ride.

6. Leaders should know how to lead correctly and not drag the pony along. The child should feel that he/she is riding the pony and is not totally reliant on the leader (unless the child is nervous or insecure). If halting or turning, the rider must be encouraged to use the correct aids; the leader should not be doing all the work.

7. With a very young or nervous child, the leader can walk beside the pony's head and

take total control. Once the child is capable of using the aids to a certain extent, the leader should walk by the pony's shoulder and encourage – by giving a couple of clicks, or tapping the pony behind the girth with his hand – the pony to walk on more freely, giving the child the feeling that he is more in control and less dependent on the leader.

7. It is the leader's responsibility to keep the correct distance of one pony's length away from the pony in front and to line up straight, leaving enough room between each pony.

Never be in a hurry to get a child off the leading rein. A leader gives a child confidence and, without one, children can feel very vulnerable (and they are). A young child is at the mercy of his pony and few ponies are totally trustworthy. When a child has gained confidence and you feel that the moment is right and the pony is suitable, you can ask the leader to remove the lead rope and walk beside the pony (ready to take hold of the reins again if necessary).

> "Give the children a challenge but let them feel they are achieving."
> **Katherine Painter**

EXPLAIN YOURSELF CLEARLY

Take extra care to explain yourself clearly when dealing with children and make sure they understand all instructions. Remember that a young child has a limited vocabulary, so you need to choose your words carefully, using expressions that all the children can comprehend. You need to teach them specific equestrian terms (see next chapter), but also put them into 'child language' for total clarity. Explain any words you think they may not fully understand.

You could preface your instructions by a command such as, 'Now, wait until I tell you,' or 'Now, listen carefully until I tell you ...'.

TEACHING STYLE

Just as every child is an individual, so is every instructor. It is not for me to tell people exactly how they must teach but the following points are crucial.

1. After each lesson, your pupils should feel that they have been taught something.

2. Try to be firm but kind and fair.

3. Be happy with little improvements – small things can be great achievements.

4. Be positive. Home in and praise the things a child **can** do rather than concentrate on the things he can't.

5. Never pick out one child and make it an example. Children will compete amongst themselves anyway.

6. Don't be pressurised by others over lesson content or a child's progress.

7. Be enthusiastic!

3 TEACHING THE BASICS

THE ARENA

Before you proceed with the lesson it is important that the children are aware of the arena and the markers they are to ride round.

Depending on their ages, you can use a rhyme or mnemonic to help them memorise the order

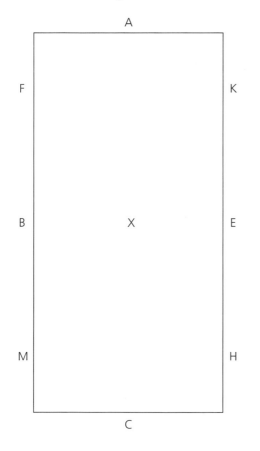

of the letters round the school. For example:

Clockwise

All King Edward's Horses Can Manage Big Fences

or

All Kind Elephants Have Cuddly Mothers, Big Fathers

Anti-clockwise

All Furry Black Mother Cats Have Eight Kittens

There is scope to play a game where the children think up a rhyme themselves – always highly entertaining!

RIDING TERMS

Here are some riding terms which may need clarifying for children:

Leading file – the rider at the front of the ride

Rear file – the rider at the back of the ride

Whole ride – all the riders together

Go large – ride round the outside of the school

Halt – stop

Change the rein – go across the school so you change from going round to the right, to going to the left, or the other way round

Whole ride, inwards turn and halt – everyone turns their pony towards the middle of the school and then stops, so they form a straight line facing the centre of the school

Up the centre – turn up the middle line of the school which runs from A to C

Run up your stirrups – slide the stirrup irons up the inside leather to the top so they are safe for leading the pony

Make much of your ponies – give them a good pat

On the right rein/left rein – the direction you go round the school. Right rein is clockwise, left rein is anti-clockwise

CHOOSING A LEADING FILE

The choice depends on the ability of the children. Explain the role of the leading file and, in the case of the riders off the leading rein, that the leading file must keep an eye on the rest of the ride and neither leave them behind nor get too far ahead. Children like to be given responsibility.

On leading rein
Choose the most experienced leader, or the pony appearing to be the liveliest (such a pony is

more likely to settle at the front of the ride than at the back).

Off leading rein or a combination
Choose the most competent rider (you may have to change, but at least you are giving that rider a challenge). Remember to cater for all levels of ability; try to give each rider his fair share and not just concentrate on the lower ability riders.

You can change leading files once the ride gets going. Children love to be leading file and by giving each child a turn, you give them hope and encouragement. Do not use the same leading file throughout unless the ride suffers unduly when you change to other members of the ride who cannot make their ponies go forward when in the lead.

By all means use your best rider as leading file to set an example, but do not compare him or her with the others in the ride. This can lead to feelings of utter dejection in the rest of the ride. Children should feel that they are 'all in it together' and not being compared. Children will subconsciously compete among themselves anyway but this is healthy competition and invariably engenders enthusiasm and courage.

KEEPING THE DISTANCE

Explain about keeping the correct distance (one pony's length) between them – 'If you can't see the pony's heels in front of you, you are too close. If you can see a lot of ground between you and the pony in front, you are too far away.' Although it may not be possible to keep correct distances with ponies walking at different speeds, the children should learn to be aware of the need to keep their distance and certainly not get too close.

Ponies walk at different speeds, so invariably there will be some that get left behind and have to catch up. You can either tell the ride to halt and allow the others to close up or allow the stragglers to have an extra trot (if they are capable) or tell them to cut across the school to catch up.

THE AIDS

Stopping, starting and turning are fundamental skills that every rider needs to learn from the outset. There are many different exercises and games that you can do with the children to practise these, time and time again. Chapter 6 contains a selection to choose from. You can very easily use a variation on any of the themes.

Explain that the reins are for guiding the pony and not for holding on. Explain to the children about stopping (halting), starting and turning. Ask them where the ponies' 'engines' are and how the messages get from the rider to the pony. Children like to be involved and enjoy questions and answers provided that the sessions are not prolonged nor the questions too difficult.

Q: What are the aids?

A: The aids are what you use to ask your pony to slow down, go faster, stop and turn.

Q: What aids does the rider have?

A: Legs, hands, body and voice. Whips, spurs and martingales are called 'artificial aids'.

Q: What do you do when you want your pony to stop or slow down?

A: You sit tall in the saddle and squeeze on the reins. You do not lean back or pull because if you do, your pony will pull back – and who do you think is stronger?

Q: How do you make your pony go forward?

A: You use your legs by giving a nudge with your lower leg. If your pony does not respond, then you increase the nudge to a little kick until the pony does as he is asked.

Explain that it is important to make the pony go by using your legs and that if you use a whip it may irritate the pony and make him buck (although the whip is used at times to reinforce the leg).

Q: How do you ask your pony to turn?

A: You squeeze (pull very, very gently) on the rein on the side you wish him to go and guide him by using your opposite (outside) leg and looking where you want to go.

Little refinement of the aids can be expected at this stage. Pulling on one rein and using the opposite leg is enough for young heads to cope with. The exercises in Chapter 6 will help with co-ordination, which will improve with time and practice.

COMMON POSITION FAULTS IN THE CHILD RIDER

Sitting with the lower leg too far back.

Slumping the upper body.

- Children are never too young to learn the right way to do things. From an early age they should learn that the rein is like elastic.

- They must learn never to be harsh and to respect their ponies.

- As they ride, urge them to sit up and use the aids correctly.

- A child's position will improve automatically as he finds his balance and his weight drops down into his foot, i.e. the weight is always in the stirrup.

• 'Eyes first' is a good catch-phrase. They should sit up and look where they are going – just as they should when riding their bicycles!

> "Teach them what you want them to know as an adult. Children are individuals – like horses – and you need to build up a rapport." **Maureen Chamberlain**

IMPROVING POSITIONS

Most children will sit correctly once they have mastered their balance on the pony but there are some children whose posture needs improvement. Here are a few ideas to help get the message across.

A **leaf** tucked into the rider's hat is an invaluable aid in helping keep the head up. If the child looks down, the leaf will flop forward and the child will be able to see it. If the child keeps his head up, he will not be able to see the leaf! (If you do not have absolutely the right prop with you, improvise. In fact, children love looking for props, so you can send them off to find leaves (for example) for these exercises.)

A **glove** or a **bean-bag** placed on top of the rider's head is another method of helping to keep the head up.

A **leaf** placed under the rider's bottom stops them wriggling about and makes them sit still. (This is also a useful exercise for the more advanced pupil doing sitting trot or canter.)

A fun exercise to help keep the heels down is to place some **sand** or **earth** on the end of the child's toe. You can have a competition to see who can keep it on the longest. If you have the same child winning or losing, you can cheat a little with the amount of sand you use and where you put it! Remember, you need always to encourage and not dishearten.

A little heap of sand, strategically placed on the toe of the rider's foot, provides a fun exercise which helps to keep the heels down.

LUNGEING

Used in moderation, this can be a very useful teaching aid. Being on the lunge means that the child does not have to worry about controlling the pony and can therefore concentrate on his riding position.

- You need to be sure that the pony is well behaved on the lunge.

- Always lunge the pony without the rider first, even if you think know the pony well. Even the most docile pony has been known to pop in a buck when first released on the lunge.

- Remember that lungeing pushes a child to the outside and you have to be careful with a small child that he is strong enough in his seat to withstand this force.

- Only lunge for short periods of time because

> "Enjoy first, learn second."
> **Sarah Charles**

it is intensive work and tiring.

- Children enjoy the novelty of being lunged.

- Provided that the pony is very quiet, on the lunge is an ideal time for mounted exercises.

- As the child progresses, work without stirrups is extremely beneficial.

- Work on the lunge is excellent for the more competent rider up to the highest level.

4 STARTING AND FINISHING A LESSON

Introducing yourself to the ride is an integral part of the lesson and is necessary for whatever age group you are teaching. Making your pupils feel relaxed and important as individuals, however well they ride or smart their pony, means that you are building up a rapport from the outset.

Here are a variety of ways of getting a lesson started.

Don't spend too long on the introductions, nor the tack check, otherwise the children's attention will start wandering before the lesson gets going. Remember to introduce yourself to any leaders as well as to the riders.

It depends on where you are teaching whether you supervise the tacking up (doing your tack check at the same time) or whether the ponies are produced tacked up and ready by the parents/helpers. Explain whether you want the children already mounted before they come into the school, or whether you would prefer the ponies led in, ready to be mounted. Either way, make sure the ride is controlled and disciplined before you line them up.

It is probably preferable to have the children already on board, provided they have adequate help, because it takes time to get six children organised and mounted. You can practise mounting later on in the lesson if appropriate.

WEATHER CONSIDERATIONS

When you check out your teaching area, identify areas of shelter or shade. In some cases there may be very little, but use what there is.

Line your ride up to the best advantage and do not have them standing around for too long in wet or cold weather.

If the weather is foul and the lesson is still going ahead, warn the parents that the lesson may be shorter than specified. You are not shirking!

TACK AND RIDER CHECK

Always carry out a tack (and rider) check before you start teaching. You will soon see if the tack is likely to be in need of repair from the general state of it and the overall turnout of pony and rider.

Tack check
1. Look for **correctly fitting tack**. The saddle should fit pony and rider so that the child is

put in a balanced position. Strategically placed foam pads can help transform a saddle that tips a child out of balance. If the saddle is totally unsuitable, you should inform the child's parents (if appropriate). Although they may not be in a position to buy a new saddle, there are secondhand ones available at reasonable prices. There is now an excellent range of synthetic saddles for ponies at competitive prices, and some manufacturers give free, expert advice on fitting.

2. Check fitting and suitability of the pony's **bit**.

3. **Nosebands** should be fitted correctly. Check that any flash noseband is not fitted too low. Often these are fitted so that the lower strap interferes with the pony's breathing or the cavesson part pinches the skin by the bit.

Stainless-steel safety stirrup with elastic band on the outside.

Correctly fitted flash noseband which does not restrict the pony's breathing.

4. Carefully check the **stirrup irons**. Children should always use safety stirrups, made of stainless steel. They should never use a nickel iron. Nickel, being a soft metal, will bend. If the rider's foot is crushed in a fall, the iron can bend, trapping the foot, which is highly dangerous and may lead to the rider getting dragged.

Safety irons are absolutely crucial on a saddle with stirrup bars in the form of a fixed D – often found on felt saddles. The elastic of the safety stirrup should always be on the outside of the stirrup because the child can still get his foot stuck if the elastic is on the inside.

Watch out for stirrup irons that are too big. These can be equally dangerous because they can allow the child's foot to slip right through the stirrup.

5. Do not assume that the **stirrups are level**. Always check by standing in front of the pony and also make sure that the saddle is sitting centrally. The stirrup leathers should be specifically designed for children and not be too thick or bulky or so long that there is excess spare leather hanging down.

6. Check the length of **leathers**. A child has not the strength to ride long, but an over-short stirrup makes it difficult for the child to use his or her legs effectively. A good guide is that the child should ride at jumping length; riding longer makes balance more difficult to master.

7. If the tack is old and handed down – and there's nothing wrong with that – check that the **stitching is safe**, especially on the reins and stirrup leathers (the most common areas

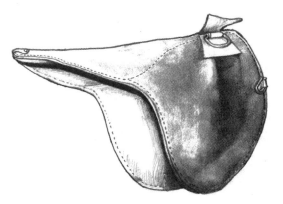

Pony pad with fixed Ds for the stirrup leathers. Safety irons are imperative for this type of fitting.

BELOW LEFT: Rider testing length of stirrups by standing up in them, as if for rising trot. Whilst he has managed to find a good balance, these leathers would be on the long side for a child of his age/strength/experience. Generally, leathers that are too long make balance difficult and produce a weak lower leg position.

BELOW RIGHT: Stirrups too short, forcing the rider's knee off the front of the saddle, making it difficult for him to use his legs effectively.

for weak stitching). Check that the tack is not brittle. Old tack is fine provided it has not been neglected. Leather that has been allowed to dry out never fully recovers despite liberal oiling.

8. Check the **girth** and **girth straps**. Make sure they are not worn. Check that the girth can be tightened sufficiently. (Some ponies require two lengths of girth to accommodate a fluctuating waist-line!) The girth should not be so long that the buckles are right under the child's leg. This can be very uncomfortable and may cause bruising to the child's knee.

9. Every pony should have a **neck-strap**. This is to help teach the rider about balance, and is something to hold onto when trotting, cantering or jumping. Ensure that the neck-strap is sufficiently tight so that it does not swivel round the pony's neck as the child holds it. The strap itself should not be too wide or bulky for small fingers to manage, nor should it be so tight that the child has to lean forward to hold onto it. The neck-strap can be secured to the saddle Ds with string to prevent it sliding down the pony's neck. A stirrup leather can improvise as a neck-strap and the loose end can be kept tidy with a large elastic band.

10. Long **reins** should be knotted short to avoid the child falling off the back of the pony. However, do make sure there is no chance of the child getting his foot caught in the spare loop when the reins are knotted – use a double knot if necessary to reduce the size of the loop. If the reins are knotted, be careful that the pony cannot snatch downwards because a small child can easily be pulled over the pony's head.

11. **Grass reins** are useful as an aid to control. Some ponies will already have them fitted.

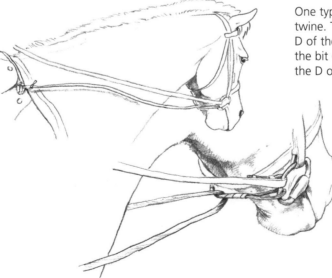

One type of grass rein fitting, with baler twine. The twine passes from the front D of the saddle through a coupling on the bit (cord works well) and back to the D on the other side.

FITTING GRASS REINS

There are a variety of ways of fitting grass reins. String works perfectly well although proper leather grass-reins do look smarter.

1. Run a piece of string from the front D of the saddle through the back of the noseband and then back to the D on the other side of the saddle.

2. Run two pieces of string from the front D of the saddle down through a loop of the brow band to the ring of the bit. The pony is then free to move his head and neck but is prevented from eating grass or snatching downwards.

3. Run two pieces of string from the front Ds on the saddle, crossing at the withers, to the bit ring on the opposite side.

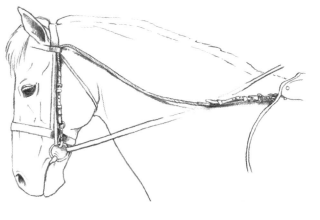

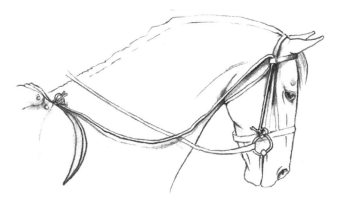

More examples of grass reins.

TOP: A custom-made leather grass-rein attached each side to the bit and the D ring of the saddle.

MIDDLE: Custom-made leather grass-rein passing each side from the bit, up through the brow band to the D of the saddle.

BOTTOM: Twine used as an alternative to the leather in the same way as the one above.

Others may need string to create some. Always check that the pony has had them fitted before and that it does not object to them before you put them on. Always err on the loose side initially.

Details of how to fit grass reins are given on the previous page.

12. For a saddle that slips, you could suggest the use of a **breastgirth** or **breastplate** for one that slides back, or a **crupper** for one that slips up the pony's neck. Another useful piece of equipment is Nicho-Net, a lightweight foam net used by many racehorse trainers to stop the saddle slipping, which can be placed under the saddle to great effect.

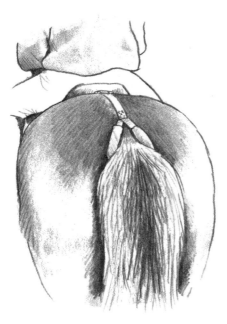

A correctly fitted crupper, which prevents the saddle from slipping forward up the pony's neck. It also prevents the saddle from slipping round to a great extent on a rather roly-poly pony.

Rider check

1. **Hats** – Make sure the hat is correctly fitted. Check that it cannot tip forward onto the child's nose by making sure that the harness is fitted snugly. The hat should not move unduly on the child's head. (See also page 18.)

2. **Footwear** – either a jodhpur boot, or a stout shoe with a flat sole and small heel, is suitable, especially with safety stirrups.

3. No child should be allowed to ride in **earrings**. If caught on a branch or twig, these can tear and damage the ear.

4. If a child is wearing **glasses**, check that the lens are, as for other sports, either plastic or shatter-proof glass. Check that the glasses are secure and not loose-fitting.

5. Encourage the wearing of **gloves**. If a child is used to wearing gloves from an early age, it will become part of his 'uniform' of riding. The gloves should not be bulky. Not only do gloves protect the rider's hands, they also allow more 'feel' due to the rider not having to clench his fist to keep hold of the reins.

6. Young children should not carry **whips** initially. It will be enough for them to manage to hold the reins without worrying about holding a whip as well. They will not be able to use a whip correctly anyway until they can ride quite competently. However, once a child can cope with the reins, it is a good idea to get him used to carrying a whip, without using it, so that he is prepared for when the time comes that he does need one. Many whips

Whip with elastic bands wrapped around the handle to improve the grip.

their hand by the loop. These loops are best cut off to avoid any temptation of the hand being put through it, and either a rubber martingale stop placed at the top of the whip, or several thick elastic bands placed at intervals on the handle to aid grip.

7. Although it may be obvious, check that the child's **jodhpurs** fit and that they are not too tight in the leg or the crutch.

8. **Half chaps** are a good idea provided that they fit comfortably. They give a child extra grip and support.

have loops on the handle. Never allow a child to use this. These loops, although preventing the child from dropping the whip, can cause unpleasant accidents if the whip gets caught on an object such as a fence or the branch of a tree. Also, many children have broken their wrists by falling off with the whip attached to

Well-fitting half chaps with jodhpur boots.

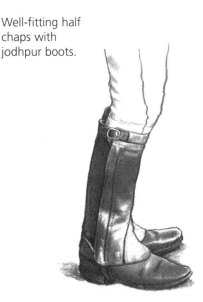

A neat, well-turned-out rider, ready for action.

9. In hot weather, insist that the children have **long sleeves**. Not only does this give protection against a hot sun, it also gives some protection against grazes should they fall off.

10. If you have to teach in the rain, make sure the children's **wet-weather gear** is suitable and that they are not wearing the sort of nylon coat that can flap and crackle in the wind. Most ponies would object to this.

11. If a child is wearing a **coat**, insist that it is done up. The principle should be drummed in from the beginning: 'If you wear a coat, do it up, or take it off.'

Note: Body protectors are obligatory for children in the Pony Club for cross-country riding. It is up to parents whether they are worn for general riding.

IF THE RIDERS ARE UNFAMILIAR TO YOU

- Take your ride in an orderly, single-file manner to your allotted area (which you have already seen and marked out with your markers as necessary).

- Make sure the gate is shut and fastened securely.

- Line them up to introduce yourself to them, and the riders to each other if necessary. By lining them up, you are setting the standard of discipline. A good way of 'breaking the ice' is to ask them to introduce themselves to each other, which gets them talking; it also helps

the shy ones because they have to join in. You need to start off with some general chit-chat just to relax the children. It is a personal choice whether the children should call you by your first name or more formally (however, if you are teaching at Pony Club or at a riding establishment, it is worth asking if they have a policy about this).

- Find out about the children's ponies: name, age, colour, sex – thus the class is already learning about colours and the names for mares and geldings. You could even talk about a pony's breeding if you have an obvious breed specimen– say, a Shetland – in the group.

- You can further familiarise yourself with each child and pony as you go down the line checking the tack. You can ask the children what sort of noseband their pony is wearing, or about the pony's bit.

- Explain to the leaders and the ride what they are going to do.

IF YOU ALREADY KNOW THE CHILDREN ON THE RIDE

If you know your ride is capable of mounting, or being given a leg up, it is good discipline and practice for them to lead their ponies into the school and line up in an orderly fashion before being told to get on.

- Line up the children (this re-emphasises the discipline of lining up) and say 'Hello' and

'How are you?'

- Ask how their ponies are, and if the children have had a good week at school, good holiday or whatever, just to get them chatting and part of the group.

- Have a quick look at the tack, checking girths, stirrup lengths, neck-straps, hats, etc. just in case the tacking up was done a little hastily.

- Jog memories on colours of the ponies or breeds.

- Ask simple questions to draw the children into the lesson and get their attention.

- Explain to the leaders and the ride what they are going to do.

EXERCISE: INTRODUCTIONS ON THE MOVE

This exercise is for children and ponies who are well known to you – you must have amenable ponies which will accept riders putting out their arms and which do not kick. It makes a good start to a lesson when the weather is chilly and you want to get moving as soon as possible.

- Line-up the ride.

- Greet the riders and leaders.

- Complete a quick tack and girth check.

- Explain to the leaders and the ride what they are going to do.

- Divide the ride in two. Ask them which hand they use to shake hands (the right one). Explain that they must therefore pass right hand to right hand as they ride round the school (remind them that it is normally left hand to left hand when riding in a school.) Choose two leading files and send the two rides off in opposite directions around the school in walk.

- Stop the ride and explain how to hold reins in one hand.

- As they pass each other ask them to stop, put reins in left hand and shake right hands with each other.

- Change rein and repeat exercise.

Aim and benefits

- Children thoroughly enjoy this exercise.

- It provides immediate activity.

- It is a good warm-up for riders.

- It teaches control – holding the reins in one hand as well as steering, stopping and making pony walk on again.

- It encourages children to look ahead.

- It relaxes a tense rider by giving plenty to think about and do.

Teaching points

- Keep alert for any pony showing signs of aggression.

- Be careful not to allow the exercise to go on

for too long.

- Use only experienced leaders.

- Never attempt this with a nervous pony or one likely to kick.

FINISHING A LESSON OR RIDE

Children can become quite excitable during lessons, especially if they include mounted games or jumping. As it is best not to hand an over-active bunch of children back to their parents, a wind-down period is important.

You can choose a variety of options to settle everyone back down after an exhilarating time.

1. Mounted exercises whilst the ponies stand still.

2. Riding at walk without stirrups.

3. Questions and answers.

4. Stable management – including what they must do to their ponies when they have finished riding them.

5. Practising dismounting and mounting.

6. Practising running up stirrups, loosening girth and taking reins over the ponies' heads.

7. Practising leading their ponies.

8. Refreshment time – a reward for riding well? Always popular!

9. Finally, praise the riders and ask them to praise their ponies (making much). They should then dismount, run up their stirrups, loosen the girth, take the reins over the pony's head and lead off in single file in an orderly fashion, maintaining the correct distance.

5 THINGS TO DO IN MID-LESSON BREAKS

REFRESHMENT BREAK

Riding is hard work and children quickly become tired both mentally and physically. What appears to be very undemanding as far as we are concerned has a very different effect on a child. Having a drink (not fizzy!) and something to eat recharges the batteries and you can proceed with the next stage of the lesson with a more responsive child.

Not every occasion allows for a refreshment break. At a riding school, for instance, such a break would be most unlikely, so you need to check this beforehand.

If the lesson is short then a 'bun time' is something for them to look forward to at the end. With a regular group this time becomes a key part of the lesson, particularly once you have discovered the children's favourite snack. Iced buns are a big part of the Fernie Pony Club and it is amazing how older members look back very fondly on those refreshment times!

It is important, though, to make this a disciplined time.

Break-time

- Find a suitable place.

- Make sure the ride is correctly lined up.

- The children must dismount properly, and run up their stirrups. They should not just abandon their ponies to rush to the goodies!

- It makes a good break for the children if you have holders for the ponies so that your pupils have a 'change of scenery' and are then more enthusiastic about getting back on.

If the weather is cold...

- You could give the children some lively games to warm them up, such as running round the school and touching various objects. It is very difficult for children to keep warm when riding because they are mostly so passive. To warm them up you need to think of fun activities for them to do.

If the weather is very hot...

- Encourage the children to remove their hats, putting them somewhere safe where they will not get trodden on. This is a good time to emphasise to them how important it is not to drop their hats. If a crash cap is dropped, it can cause extensive damage, which affects its protection, and would then necessitate purchasing a new one.

• Make sure you find a shady area for break-time and make sure the children have plenty to drink.

• Some cold water for them to splash on their faces or a damp cloth which helps cool them down is a good idea.

STABLE MANAGEMENT BREAK

While the children are off their ponies you can use the time for some stable management tuition.

Careful supervision is necessary at all times when small, inexperienced children are handling ponies in any way. A child can easily be trodden on, knocked or pulled over.

A child is not physically strong and small children should only be allowed to handle kind, sensible, well-mannered ponies but even so, they should not be left unsupervised.

Without seeming to be full of doom and gloom, do remind children of the safety aspects of handling ponies.

From an early age, the child should be taught:

• How to hold a pony.

• Not to let it loose unless someone has taken

With the assistance of the instructor, the pupil is checking his girth

stirrups when you are leading or holding a pony (a) the pony may, by trying to have a scratch, get the iron caught in its mouth, or (b) the stirrup could catch on something when the pony is being led.

- How to lead into a stable or through a gateway, taking care that the pony is straight and does not catch his hips in the doorway.

- How to put on or remove a headcollar.

- How to tie up by using a quick-release knot.

Lifting up the saddle flap to tighten the girth. The instructor should check that the girth is tight enough, correctly fastened and the buckle guard is in place.

hold of the reins or lead rope.

- How to lead correctly.

- How to tighten the girths (even though a small child is not strong enough to do it).

- Run up the stirrups – and why you run up the

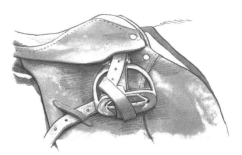

Often, very short stirrups will not remain run up. Secure them by twisting the leather round the iron and then passing the end of the leather through the loop at the bottom.

The correct way to lead a pony out of a stable. The pony, not the leader, should be central to the doorway to prevent the pony from catching either the stirrups or his hips on the doorway.

A FEW WORDS OF CAUTION FOR YOUR RIDERS

• *'Do not walk behind your pony.'*

• *'Never startle a pony – always speak before touching.'*

• *'Never kneel, only squat beside a pony. If the pony jumped, you could not move out of the way quickly enough from a kneeling position.'*

• *'Never wrap the lead rope around your hand.'*

• *'Always tie up to a single piece of baler twine.'*

• *'Never kiss your pony on the nose, however much you love him. He may think your nose is a carrot….'*

Why that kind of knot is necessary, as well as why you always tie up to string as opposed to something solid (if the pony gets the rope caught or pulls back, it is vital the string breaks, otherwise the headcollar breaks, or disastrously, the pony's neck).

• How to put on and remove everyday tack.

• Always to shut gates/stable doors.

• The principles of mucking out.

• The very basic principles of feeding and watering.

• How (in very simple terms) you age a pony.

Children love questions and answers and this is a good way to introduce them to stable management theory. Here are some ideas for mini stable management lessons.

You can divide your ride into teams or work individually, whichever seems more appropriate.

1. **Points of the pony** are always popular. Make sure you choose a very quiet pony because however much you tell the children not to rush to touch various parts, in their excitement they will forget. The pony must be very long-suffering. Sticky labels with a name of a point of the horse written on, which the children have to stick in place is a favourite game.

2. If you have been allotted a long teaching session then you will have time to practise **putting a bridle together**. Have the parts of a snaffle bridle in a bucket and ask each child to take out a piece and decide what it is. Then assemble the bridle. You could incorporate tack cleaning, if time, with each child cleaning one piece of the bridle. This is not as daunting for them as cleaning a whole bridle and they really enjoy cleaning their one piece.

CAUTION: Never allow a child to squat in front of a pony – explain that if the pony had a fright and jumped forward, the child would be knocked over and probably injured.

3. Teach the **parts of the saddle** too. You can use sticky labels to make it more fun. Each child has to stick a label with the name of part of the saddle in the correct place. (Make sure the saddle has not too much saddle soap on it or the labels will not stick.)

4. **Grooming** is always a popular pastime for stable management. Provide a grooming kit and ask the children to name the items and explain their uses. Then ask the children to use them.

5. **Colours and markings** – with luck you will have a good selection amongst your ride. You can draw markings on a pony in chalk or ask the children to draw a particular marking.

6. The **tray memory game** is fun. Have a selection of items on a tray or stable rubber, such as a horseshoe, brush, over-reach boot, hoof-pick etc. Give the children a minute to memorise the objects and then remove the items. Ask the children to name them. This can be a team game too, but pick your teams carefully so that they are evenly matched.

7. Introduce the children to such items as boots, martingales and other **basic tack** – children like to touch things so allow them all to be hands on.

8. Other topics you can cover are **poisonous plants.** You could provide some examples.

(Make sure they are in plastic bags so that the children do not handle them directly. Dispose of them carefully.)

9. Show different types of **bedding**.

10. Show different types of **feed**. Try to provide some examples if possible, or photographs.

11. Children like **picking out feet** (be careful of toes getting trodden).

12. **Bandaging** is always popular and great fun! Stress, though, that they should leave bandaging to an adult. (Use a very quiet pony as the guinea pig.) Explain the dangers of exercise bandages and that they should never use them.

13. Provide a box of various '**bits and bobs**' and get each child to pick out something and discuss it.

14. Give each child a piece of **paper and pencil**. Each child has to draw an object and the rest have to guess what it is.

15. You can show how to recognise if a pony is **lame**. Make one of the children pretend to be lame. Explain about the horse nodding his head when the sound leg hits the ground.

16. **Practise leading ponies**. Demonstrate how you must run up the stirrups, take the reins over the ponies' heads, and the correct way to hold the reins when you lead. Demonstrate the

correct and incorrect way to turn when you are leading. (This is done ideally with a big dog. In that way there is no danger of any toes being trodden on, but it must be a good-tempered, long suffering dog!) Most ponies will need to have grass reins on if you are practising leading on grass. Always be on hand to help if the pony gets strong. Make sure the children have stout shoes on – wellies or trainers do not give enough protection if the pony (particularly a shod one) treads on their toes.

17. Draw **a large picture of a horse**. On another piece of paper, write down as many points of the horse, markings, and conformation defects that you can think of and cut them out. Affix a small bit of Blue-tack onto the reverse side of these and place them face down on a tray. Each child in turn chooses a label and then sticks it on the relevant part of the horse. If the child does not know where to place it or puts it in the wrong place, ask the other children if they know. Then replace the label on the tray and mix it up with the other labels so that the children will have chance to remember the next time the piece is picked up. This game can either be played individually or in teams and is fun as well as being educational.

Keep any stable management session short. You have far more chance of the children remembering something, at least, if they do not lose interest. Stable management can be incredibly dull to a child (I remember that from my own childhood!) so try to use as many

games as possible as a means to learning and remembering and keep the children involved.

Keep the subject matter simple and uncomplicated and suitable for the particular age group. There is nothing more boring than being bombarded with information you cannot understand and which makes no sense.

Do not allow your refreshment time and/or stable management time to drift on too long. Keep each different activity to the allotted time in your planning otherwise you will find the children will lose interest in the riding side of things.

At the end of the break, get hats back on, check that none of the children need to 'spend a penny' and then get them mounted again. This then presents a suitable moment to practise getting on and off.

This can be part of a mounted exercise session, and now, after the refreshment break, is possibly a good moment to do it.

MOUNTING AND DISMOUNTING

To help the smaller child or one with a big pony, you can use a crate to help them reach the stirrup.

Let the children practise getting on and off both sides.

Show the children how to hold the reins properly before they mount and try to impress that they should land lightly in the saddle.

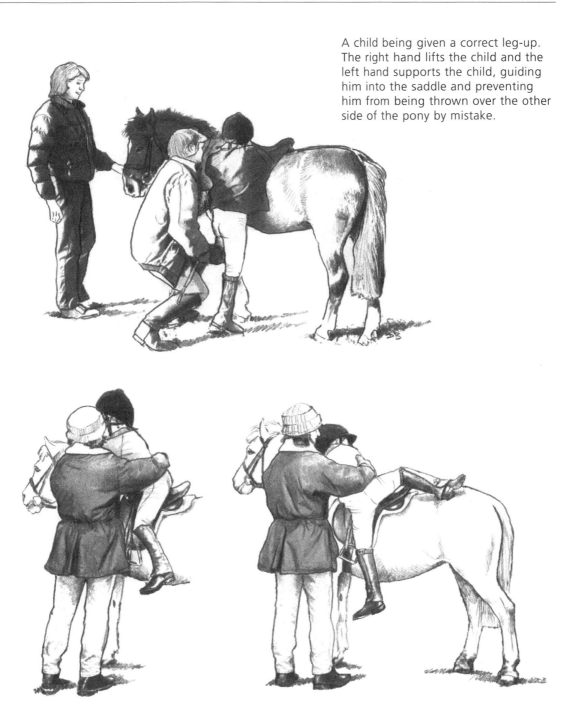

A child being given a correct leg-up. The right hand lifts the child and the left hand supports the child, guiding him into the saddle and preventing him from being thrown over the other side of the pony by mistake.

Helping a child to dismount by supporting and guiding to prevent the child from kicking the pony on the bottom and from over-balancing and falling over on landing.

Using a mounting block to mount, with a helper holding the pony to prevent it from moving away.

For those who are too small to mount, practise the leg-up with a leader. Show the leader how to support the child around the tummy as you lift the child into the saddle. The child should try to spring off the leg on the ground, which prepares for mounting when the time comes.

Stress how important it is to take both feet out of the stirrups before dismounting.

Be ready to support a child when he dismounts.

Often, the child may lose his balance and stagger backwards, particularly when dismounting from the offside.

MOUNTED EXERCISES AT HALT/WALK

Mounted exercises can be slotted in at any stage of a teaching session. You can even start your lesson with basic stretching exercises if it fits into your plan. It is a good way of getting the children loosened up and should be part of every lesson in one way or another. Suppleness and relaxation are a vital part of riding at every level and should not be considered old-fashioned or boring.

Mounted exercises are a good way to help warm up the children if the weather is chilly and they are beginning to get cold.

They can help improve security, suppleness, balance, rider position and confidence, and can be done with any standard of ride.

Make sure all the ponies are held, and with the smaller children you may even need two people per child for some exercises – one to hold the pony and the other to supervise the child.

If you have only one helper per pony, then you may need to do the activities one at a time so that you are there to catch hold of the child if he or she loses balance.

Some of these exercises can be done on the move, but always have a leader for any exercise that could compromise the safety of the child.

Until you know the possible reaction of the ponies, **it is vital to start with the ride stationary.** You can then do some simple exercises on the move if you think it is appropriate.

You can use 'Simon Says' as part of your exercises – the children really enjoy the challenge of being caught out (even more so if someone else is caught out!).

With children who know you, these exercises are often a highlight of the lesson. You can make them such fun (but all the time you are teaching).

As you run through all the exercises, you invariably build up a sequence which the children reckon they know – but they love that. Children love familiarity and repetition.

All exercises are best done at the halt initially and some at a later stage at walk. Only with a secure, confident child would you contemplate doing them at a faster pace.

Teaching points

- Have plenty of helpers to lead the ponies, or steady the riders.

- Assess the ride. The ponies must be safe and settled. Always have leaders if you are unsure about any of the ponies.

- Knot the reins and tell the children to hold onto the saddle or neck-strap. (It depends on the standard of the ride whether they quit and cross their stirrups.)

- Start with very easy exercises.

- Make your instructions very clear to avoid misunderstandings and demonstrate what you want them to do.

- Correct their positions but give plenty of praise and encouragement, especially to the less athletic child.

- If a pony objects, tell the child to stop doing that particular exercise.

- A more capable ride could do some of these exercises at trot, provided their ponies will keep a regular rhythm and neither speed up nor cut across the school. The leading file, however, must keep hold of his reins and maintain the pace.

- These exercises are very useful for work on the lunge (see Lungeing, pages 29–30).

Examples

With/without stirrups

1. Shrug shoulders.

2. Turn head slowly from side to side.

3. Put hands on hips and turn upper body slowly from side to side.

4. Hands in the air – one at a time, then both together, stretching up.

5. Put arms out sideways and turn upper body slowly from side to side – playing aeroplanes.

MOUNTED EXERCISES

Pulling the lower leg up to stretch the thigh muscles.

Lying back on the pony, an exercise which encourages trust, relaxation and suppleness, as well as testing the security of the rider's lower leg, which here has moved forwards slightly and the heel has come up.

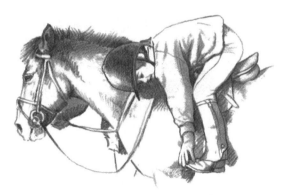

Bending down to touch the toe.

Touching the other toe. Note how the lower leg has lost position – a common fault.

6. Hold ankle, bend knee and bring lower leg up to meet thigh, first on one side then the other.

7. Touch parts of the pony's body.

8. Do actions in quick succession. For example: 'Are you all ready? Right, whole ride put your hands on your head, hands on your shoulders, your knees, your tummy, behind your back, on your head, on your tummy,' etc. and see how quickly you can get the children

reacting. This is a game they love. It tests their balance as they do the various movements and improves suppleness and relaxation.

9. Put hands on hips and swing upper body forward – the riders must look between their ponies' ears, keep their lower leg still and their heels down – 'Eyes up, heels down!'

10. Forward swing either with hands on hips, or with arms folded, or leaning forward to touch

the pony's ears, or placing the hands either side of pony's neck.

11. Pretend to hold reins whilst attempting a forward swing – ditto above.

12. Circle arms like a windmill – first one arm, then the other, then both together. Use images to help enthuse the ride – ask 'Who can be the biggest windmill with the largest sails?'

13. Bend down and touch the right toe with the right hand, then repeat with the left side.

14. Bend down and touch right toe with left hand, then vice versa.

Stretching the legs out and down.

15. Place hands on hips or arms outstretched and turn the upper body to face first one way then the other. See if they can touch their pony's croup with one hand, and if they can bend forward to try to reach the pony's ears with the other.

With stirrups

1. Stand up in the stirrups, first holding the neck-strap, then with hands on hips.

2. Standing up in the stirrups and sitting down (softly) again.

3. Taking feet out of the stirrups and putting them back in again – 'Who can do it the quickest?' (Have a leader with any pony that may resent a child vigorously rooting for the stirrup – i.e. inadvertently giving the pony a good kick in the ribs!)

Without stirrups

1. With one hand on the saddle, stretch the other hand up into the air as far as possible, then repeat on the other side.

2. Stretch toes down to the ground.

3. Lift the knees up like a jockey and then drop them down.

4. Swing the lower legs (from the knee down) alternately forwards and backwards.

6. Arm swinging backwards and forwards from the shoulders and leg swinging backwards

'Round the world', with someone holding the pony at the head to prevent it from moving and also ready to hold the child if he loses balance.

Child must be careful not to kick the pony on the bottom as he passes his leg round the back.

and forwards from the knee, separately, together, and one forward and one back improves co-ordination. Make sure that the child does not kick the pony as he swings his legs, and that his seat does not move around in the saddle.

7. Circling the ankles – drawing circles with the toes – helps supple the ankles and warms up cold toes. Alternate the direction of the circles, as well as using one ankle at a time and both together; this improves the ability to use the limbs independently.

8. Stretch the legs down and pull up the toes to create a good leg position.

9. Round the world – every pony must have a leader who must be ready to catch the rider if he/she loses balance.

10. Half scissors – ditto above.

11. Full scissors – ditto above.

12. Arms folded, leaning back onto the pony's back then getting up again with arms still folded – ditto above.

13. Jumping on and off (children will no doubt need assistance to get on with a correct leg-up).

Putting a twist in the stirrup leathers.

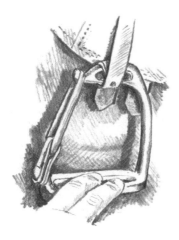

The finished twist.

PRETENDING TO BE JOCKEYS

Children love having their stirrups shortened and pretending to be jockeys. This is very good for improving their balance and is also great fun. It is very time-consuming, so bear that in mind before you embark on the lengthy process of altering all the stirrups, necessitating putting twists in the leathers in most cases.

This is also an excellent way of teaching the older child the importance of balance and fitness.

Children can also be made to realise that it is not unsafe to ride short. Far too many children ride too long and therefore unwittingly struggle with their balance. Often they start to love the feel they obtain from riding short, and once they are confident they can even jump little fences. They will find this great fun, especially if you give them jockeys' names, and they soon realise how easy it is to ride and jump short. Make sure that any fences you put up are small and easy, and will encourage the ponies to go forward. However, do explain that the reason we do not ride short all the time is that we cannot use our legs so effectively.

RIDING BAREBACK OR 'SIDE-SADDLE'

In an enclosed area with a leader, the children can ride bareback for a while. Be ready to hold a child's leg if he or she looks like slipping off. Children also love sitting 'side-saddle'. With a leader ready to hold their leg if necessary, the children can be led round in walk sitting side-saddle and also facing backwards.

Do not do this with anything other than the quietest of ponies.

All these types of exercise improve balance, security and confidence.

6 IDEAS FOR EARLY LESSONS

None of the exercises and games in this section requires anything in the way of equipment, although some poles and cones would come in handy. All you need is a marked-out arena. Remember, do not make your area too large, and if you put out cones, ensure that the ride knows they must go round them to prevent the area from rapidly diminishing!

Although most of these exercises and games are aimed at four- to nine-year olds and executed at the walk, older children could perform them in trot and would certainly benefit from practising many of them. For example, a turn down the centre line is something an advanced dressage horse has to perfect, so this is one of several exercises which can be used at all levels. Each level will be striving to achieve something different.

Whilst an instructor is often faced with teaching a ride of varying ages and abilities, it is perfectly feasible to satisfy all the children in the lesson by expecting different levels of achievement while performing various school movements and exercises. There is no reason for a more competent child to be bored in a lesson with less capable riders. This presents a challenge for the instructor, which requires prior planning; hence the importance of knowing, in advance, the standard of the pupils in a lesson.

In a subtle way, through the use of various exercises and activities, you can instil confidence in your ride and teach them to be relaxed. You want them to ride automatically, positively yet gently, to sit still and look where they are going, and to be aware of the pony they are riding.

Do not plug away at the same exercise so that the children become bored or tired. Change the theme to keep their attention and interest. Make sure you do not allow the lesson to be dull or lacking gaiety. Do not lose your enthusiasm or you will lose the children's willingness and co-operation.

GENERAL POINTS ABOUT THE EXERCISES WHICH FOLLOW

- All the exercises in this chapter are suitable to be used in either the first or second active part of the lesson for approximately 15 minutes duration. No group of children is ever the same, so what may be too long for one lot may be too short for another.

- The exercises are suitable for children on or off the leading rein.

• Always send the ride off on a specified rein so that the children eventually will learn the difference between the left and right rein around the school.

EXERCISES USING THE LETTERS ROUND THE SCHOOL

TOUCHING LETTERS

About this exercise
• The ride is sent off at walk round the school on a specified rein, in single file, with one pony's distance between.

• Each child has to touch every letter with the outside hand as the pony walks past and, as he does so, call out the name of the letter.

• Change the rein so that both hands are used.

• If the children are old enough, this can be expanded into a game where the child has to think of a word (associated with ponies or riding) beginning with that letter.

• A large ride may have to take turns to call out, unless you are happy with them all calling out at the same time. (A quiet child may go unheard if you have noisy members in the ride.)

Aims and benefits
• Children become aware of the school markers and their positions round the arena.

• Improves co-ordination.

• Helps relax a nervous child by giving him something on which to concentrate.

• Improves control of the pony.

• Improves dexterity with the reins.

• Educational and fun – helps with recognition of letters and spelling.

• Helps improve balance.

• Requires concentration.

Teaching points
• Explain to the children what you are going to ask them to do.

• Stress keeping their distances.

• Explain which hand they are to use and why.

• Check that they all know how to hold the reins correctly in one hand.

• Ask if they know in which hand their whip (if carried) should be held. Explain why it should be in the same hand as they hold the reins and why – 'If you wave a whip about it may frighten not only your pony but someone else's as well.'

• Remind them to look well ahead.

• Remind them to prepare in advance by getting their reins and whip organised in the correct hand.

• Explain that they must use their legs to keep

their ponies straight when they take the reins into one hand.

- Make sure the leaders help their riders by positioning the ponies close enough to the letters that the child is not in danger of over-balancing as he reaches for the letter (but not so close that the child knocks his leg on the school fence.)

Faults

- The child fails to touch the letter – make sure the rider is looking where he is going.

- The pony lacks steerage when the rider has the reins in one hand – rider must use more leg.

- The pony stops at the letter because the rider forgets to use his legs.

USING MARKERS TO STOP AND START

About this exercise

The rear file is instructed to halt at a named letter and then each rider, from the rear, halts at the next letter they come to. When all members of the ride have halted, tell them to note where they are in relation to the pony in front of them. When they are told to walk on, they must try to keep the same distance apart. This is a difficult exercise to do but the children enjoy the challenge. This can be done in trot with a more advanced group.

Aims and benefits

- Familiarises children with the school markers.

- Teaches control.

- Improves the use of the aids.

- Helps balance.

- Encourages children to look, think and plan ahead.

- Requires concentration.

Teaching points

- Remind the ride of the aids for stopping and walking on.

- Explain how effective the use of the body is, and that they must grow tall when they want the pony to halt.

- Teach them that they must not just pull on the reins or lean back otherwise the pony will pull back.

- Tell them to imagine the reins are a piece of elastic.

- Stress that they must be gentle and not rough.

- Remind them to plan well ahead so the pony stops when the rider's leg is level with the marker.

Faults

- Pony will not stop when asked. If you walk beside the pony's head, you can help reinforce the aids without the child realising by putting your arm in front of the pony's shoulders.

The rider is leaning back and pulling as he asks his pony to halt, with the result that the pony resists and pulls back.

Repetition should improve the problem.

- Child pulls and leans back – stress growing tall.

- Rider gets rough with the aids.

TOUCHING LETTER GAME

About this exercise

- This is not a race, but the competitive nature of children may turn it into one!

- The ride spreads out and walks round the school.

- Each rider is given the name of a letter. At the command, each rider must go to that letter, make their pony halt and the rider touch the letter.

- It depends on the ability of the ride whether they walk or trot to the letters.

Teaching points

- They must look where they are going.

- Riders must pass left hand to left hand.

- Remind them to come alongside the letter otherwise they will not be able to touch it.

- They must remember to grow tall when they ask their ponies to halt.

- If you have a particularly competent rider, make sure he has the furthest to go or make him turn so he has to touch with a specified hand.

The rider has 'grown tall' as he asks his pony to halt and the pony has halted without resistance.

Faults

- Riders overshoot the letters – they need to plan the halt sooner.

- Failing to touch the letter because they have forgotten to come up alongside.

- Child cannot turn his pony away from the others – do not allow the child to become despondent. The pony may need to be led.

CHANGING LETTERS GAME

About this exercise

Each rider is told to halt at a specific letter. They are then told to change places with another rider. For instance, rider at letter C swaps places with rider at letter A. When everyone has had a go, you can change several riders at once, reminding them that they must pass left hand to left hand to avoid collisions. This should be done in walk initially and with more capable riders in trot or even canter.

REAR FILE HALTING GAME

The rear is instructed to halt at a particular letter and the rest of the ride proceeds round the school. He waits until the ride has caught up and then moves off to take leading file. It improves judgement of how soon it is necessary to prepare for a transition as well as improving control. This can be done in walk to start with and then, depending on the standard of the ride, in trot.

SIMPLE TURNS

TURNS ACROSS THE SCHOOL

About these exercises

Children are asked to turn across the school in a variety of ways. They must listen to the instructions from the teacher so they know what they must do. When being led, the children should try to turn their ponies themselves so that it keeps their interest and they feel they are achieving something, and not just being a passenger. All these turns should be done in walk initially. Only if the children are competent enough should the exercises be attempted in trot.

Aims and benefits

- Teaches the importance and relevance of the markers.

- Teaches the basic school movements.

- Teaches various ways of turning across the school.

- Teaches different ways of changing direction.

- Encourages disciplined riding.

- Improves control.

- Emphasises the need for forward planning.

Teaching points

- Choose any combination of letters but explain what movement the children are doing by giving the correct command. For example: 'Turn across the school from E to B,' or 'Up the centre at A.' You need to tell them which way to go at the second marker and this can be made into a game (see Up the Centre, page 61).

- Remind riders that they must use their legs as they ask their pony to turn – 'Inside hand and opposite (outside) leg.'

- There are any number of combinations of letters you can use to keep the interest and provide variety:

'Change the rein across the diagonal from K to F'

'Change the rein across the short diagonal from K to B'

'From the right rein, make a half-circle from E to B'

or use three letters:

'Turn across the school from F to E then back to M'

- Explain about turning and remind the children to look where they are going – 'Eyes first'.

Eyes first!

The rider should always look in the direction he wishes his pony to go.

- Give plenty of time for the children to work out where they must turn – do not expect them to react quickly.

- Take turns so that each child has a chance to be leading file. A less experienced child or an unwilling pony may need assistance. Do not let the child struggle and become frustrated or upset that he is holding up the ride.

- Remind the children that they must straighten the pony once they have completed the turn.

- Try to make the children aware of their ponies and explain that their ponies must keep the same rhythm and pace around the turn.

UP THE CENTRE

About this exercise

This is a popular game. You stand at either A or C and then ask the ride to come up the school in single file towards you. At the last minute, hold out your hand to indicate which way the ride must go. Children love the element of surprise and you can alternate which way each child has to turn. You can also get them to call out which way they are going.

Alternatively, the children have to hold out their hands to indicate which way they intend to turn and they can also call out right or left depending on which hand they hold out.

Aims and benefits

- Keeps the children interested and entertained.
- Makes the children concentrate.
- Gives useful practice in turning up the centre.
- Makes them practice riding straight lines.
- Helps children learn left and right.

TURNS ACROSS THE SCHOOL AS A RIDE

About this exercise

It is important for the ride to listen carefully to your instructions. The children must learn to differentiate between 'Whole ride' and 'Single file'. These are basic school instructions and need to be practised regularly.

Children enjoy turning across the school as a ride and it makes them competitive as they try to keep an even line. The children relish this challenge and it makes them attentive and keen.

Aims and benefits

- Children must concentrate on the instructions given.
- Practises turning across the school.
- Helps children learn right and left.

Teaching points

- Give the correct command, 'Whole ride – that means everyone – prepare to turn across the school. Whole ride TURN.' Impress on the children that they must wait for the word of command 'TURN' before asking their ponies to turn.
- They must try to stay in a straight line, which means that some will have to kick on and others hold back a little.
- Be careful that the children do not become rough with the aids in their efforts to turn on command.
- Encourage the children to look where they are going.
- Give a clear command of the direction they must take well before they reach the other side of the school. You can vary the way they change direction to give turns in being leading file.
- You can hold out your hand to indicate the way they must turn as they cross the centre line and get them to call out the direction.

TURN UP THE CENTRE AS A RIDE

About this exercise

- The ride turns up the centre together, forming a straight line.

- Irrespective of how many there are in the ride, it can be done. If you have more than four ponies you would need to number the ride. Instruct each child to call out his number, loud and clear, starting from the leading file. 'One, two, three, etc.' You may need to get the children to do this again if they are rather timid about calling out their number. Ask the others in the ride if they can hear each other. Explain that numbers 1, 2 and 3 will turn up the centre in line on command (when you tell them) then numbers 4, 5 and 6 will turn up the centre in line on command. They must try to keep abreast.

- You can also make the ride halt their ponies in line, then move off again together. This offers a further challenge and encourages the child on a slower pony to keep up with his classmates.

Aims and benefits

- Provides a real challenge for the children as well as being fun.

- Practises control and concentration.

Teaching points

- The children will need lots of encouragement, but will also need correcting at appropriate moments. Praise especially the child who is struggling to keep up with the others. This will boost confidence and enhance the child's enjoyment.

MORE EXERCISES TO PRACTISE STOPPING AND STARTING

HALTING WITHOUT A VERBAL COMMAND

About this exercise

Instead of saying, 'Whole ride halt', you stand in the centre of the school and when you want the ride to halt, you simply put your arm in the air and then drop it down when you want them to walk on again. You can also single out an individual for this exercise.

Aims and benefits

- The children have to concentrate on keeping their ponies walking forward straight, while they keep glancing at you.

- Keeps the children's attention.

- Teaches balance and awareness of their ponies.

- Makes the children do more than one thing at a time.

- Practises the transition from halt to walk.

Teaching points

- Beware that the children do not become rough with their aids in their excitement to be the first to stop! This is good practice for children in this respect because there are many instances of exciting moments when riding. The rider must not forget to use the correct aids but must still ride correctly.

- Give good marks to the rider who stops his pony the quickest AND the most correctly.

- You might need to remind the ride of the aids to stop and start to refresh memories!

'SIMON SAYS'

About this exercise

- This exercise makes use of the well-known party game where instructions are pre-fixed with 'Simon says' – for example: 'Simon says touch your pony's mane.' However, if an instruction is given without the prefix, then the children must disregard it.

- Children love this game.

- You can vary it however you like. Depending on the age and particular interests of the children, you could rename Simon with a well-known equestrian instead.

Aims and benefits

- It is fun for the children and makes them think about something else at the same time as riding their pony.

- It makes children listen carefully and concentrate on the instructions given. (Always worth practising, whatever the age of rider!)

- You can alternate instructions in any way you want and can keep the ride amused, as well as learning, for a good length of time.

'GRANDMOTHER'S FOOTSTEPS'

About this exercise

- This is another favourite party game.

- The children have to follow you as you walk round the school, and when you stop, so must they.

- Anyone seen moving once you have stopped is 'out' – or however you want to play the game.

- Depending upon the number of children in the ride, you can have either the whole ride in a line behind you, or divide the ride into twos or threes and give everyone a chance to be in front.

Teaching points

- As with other stopping games, watch that the children do not get rough with their aids in their excitement.

EXERCISES TO IMPROVE THE RIDER'S BALANCE AND FEEL

STANDING UP IN THE STIRRUPS

About this exercise

- This is the simplest of exercises to test and improve the balance of any rider at any level. Make sure that the length of stirrup is short enough to allow the rider to stand up without bumping on the pommel. (See page 33.)

ABOVE: The rider is balancing on his toe as he stands up in his stirrups, which gives a precarious position. By dropping the weight down into the heel, the rider is now in a balanced, secure position standing up in his stirrups.

- Every pony must have a neck-strap.

- This exercise can be done at any pace, depending on the standard of the ride.

Aims and benefits

- Improves balance and suppleness of the ankle.

- An invaluable exercise in a mixed-standard lesson.

- The exercise helps prepare the child for jumping because once they have mastered balance standing in their stirrups, they will have no problems in keeping balance later when jumping.

- For children who have not mastered the rising trot, standing makes trotting so much more comfortable than bobbing about on the saddle (especially for small boys) and it also gives the child the opportunity to feel the movement of their pony's trot underneath them.

Teaching points

- With each child holding the neck-strap, tell them to stand up in their stirrups. Do this initially at halt, then in walk.

- Try to ensure that the riders' weight drops into their heels, and that they are looking up and where they are going.

- When they sit down again, explain that they must sit lightly in the saddle and not thump down.

- With an older group of children, you can

The riding position requires the same balance as when the rider stands on the ground with bent knees. With 'short' stirrups, the rider's back should be flatter and not round, and with 'longer' stirrups, the rider's hips should be more over his feet for better balance.

demonstrate how standing on the ground demands the same balanced position as when riding. The younger children will not appreciate this, but their balance will automatically improve through performing this exercise.

RIDING WITHOUT STIRRUPS

About this exercise

- Helps develop confidence, security, relaxation and balance.

- You must have a secure riding arena with a soft surface.

Teaching points

- You need to be cautious if the whole ride is off the leading rein.

- It is a good idea to leave the leading file with stirrups so your leader has maximum control. You then need to swap leading files to give everyone a chance to ride without stirrups.

- If you have any doubt about the steadiness of any of the ponies or the balance of the riders, make sure the pony is led.

- Restrict the activity to walking only (unless you feel that the more advanced riders are able to trot, in which case make sure it is done one at a time, and on the straight rather than on a corner, where balance is more easily lost).

- With a very novicey child or a bumpy pony, make sure there is a leader and that he holds onto the child's lower leg just in case the child loses balance.

- You can practise stopping, starting and turning without stirrups.

- Err on the safe side.

RIDING WITH HANDS OVER THE EYES

Aims and benefits

- This helps teach awareness and feel.

- Makes the riders think about their legs and how they keep their pony going forward.

Teaching points

- This is especially good for a ride on the leading rein but can be used for a ride off the leading rein, but in this case, the leading file needs to see where he is going, so you will need to alternate leading files.

- Keep an eye on distances to avoid any kicking.

- Draw attention to how the pony is feeling underneath the child. See if they can feel which legs are moving and whether the pony is walking faster or slower.

FEET IN AND OUT OF STIRRUPS

Taking the feet out of the stirrups and putting them back in again, without looking or using the hands, is an excellent exercise and one where practice will come in useful in the future.

Some ponies object to being dug in the ribs with a toe while the child struggles to find the stirrup, so keep an eye on any pony reacting adversely and make sure it has a leader.

Show the children if their stirrup is twisted and explain how the elastic must always be on the outside of a safety stirrup.

RIDING WITH THE REINS IN ONE HAND

Show each rider individually how to hold the reins in one hand. A small child may have difficulty holding the reins correctly, but you

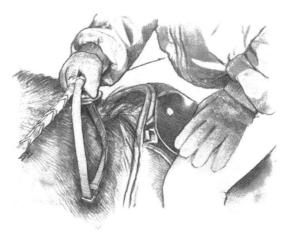

RIGHT: Holding the reins correctly in one hand.

need to explain how to hold them in one hand and how important that is (for example, how can they take something from you with the reins in two hands?) With practice, the child will be able to master it.

If any child is carrying a whip, remind him that the whip must always be in the hand with the reins to avoid inadvertently waving the whip around which would startle his own pony and possibly someone else's as well.

Aims and benefits

- A rider needs to be able to hold the reins in one hand for a multitude of different reasons and the earlier the correct way is taught, the better.

A fun thing to do is for the children to ride with the reins in, say, the left hand. Then ask them to turn right, but they cannot because they do not have a right hand on the reins. This teaches awareness of the aids as well as great amusement. (When a child is older, stronger and more effective with the leg, he will, of course, be able to turn his pony with one hand but in the initial stages of riding, he will have to rely on the inside hand to turn.)

PLAYING AN IMITATION GAME

Ask a rider to imitate an everyday action, such as playing a musical instrument or licking a lolly, and invite the rest of the ride to guess what he is doing.

Aims and benefits

- Children adore having lots of different things to do.

- This sort of activity breaks the monotony for the children as well as teaching them balance and feel.

- They must control their pony as well as doing something else – rather like patting your head and rubbing your tummy!

EXERCISES TO IMPROVE DEXTERITY AND CO-ORDINATION

PRACTISE SHORTENING AND LENGTHENING THE REINS

It is important that a child learns how to shorten his reins and also how to let them slip through his fingers. Children can be pulled over a pony's head by failing to let go of the reins when the pony puts its head down. Children find it difficult to shorten the reins and do require plenty of practice. This can be tied in with holding the reins in one hand.

CHANGING THE WHIP TO THE OTHER HAND

If any child is not carrying a whip, then he can use something else instead.

It is important that a child knows how to change a whip over. A short child's whip with a bulky end is not changed over in the same way as a dressage whip. The bulky end prevents the whip being pulled through the hand and it is impractical to change a short whip by rotating it over the pony's withers.

The reins and whip should be put into one hand, and the whip passed over the withers to the other side of the pony's neck by the free hand.

REMOVING AND REPLACING A GLOVE

This is a fun game with an opportunity for forfeits if anyone drops their glove while doing this exercise.

Each child must remove a glove, and then replace it without letting go of the reins or dropping the glove.

Mastering this art will prove extremely useful on many occasions.

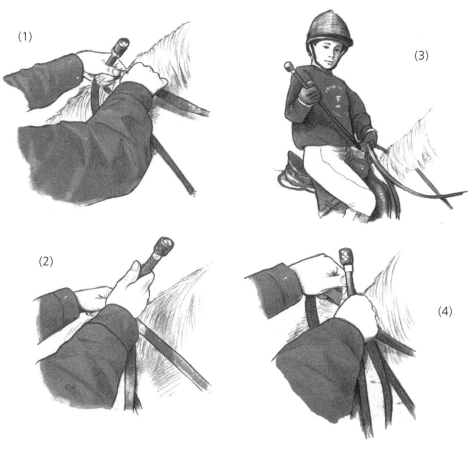

Changing the whip from left to right.

UNDOING AND DOING UP COAT BUTTONS

You can also give each child a hanky or paper tissue and get them to take it out of their pocket, pretend to use it, then replace it.

FOLLOW MY LEADER

The leading file, who must be reasonably competent, carries out a variety of simple tasks, such as riding with the reins in one hand, the other hand on his head; changing the whip from hand to hand; removing and replacing a glove, touching toes; forward swing; taking feet out of the stirrups and putting them in again, and the rest of the ride follow his lead. Children can take it in turns to be leading file but you must ensure that all the exercises are suitable for the least experienced member of the ride.

SIMPLE DRILL RIDES

RIDING IN PAIRS

About this exercise

- Divide the ride into pairs, using the colours of ponies if you can (thus some stable management information is included).

- Have the children ride various exercises in pairs, or try them on a simple drill ride.

SIMPLE DRILL RIDE

An example of a simple drill ride for eight riders

- Number the ride from the front.

- Make sure you have two relatively competent riders to be numbers 1 and 2.

- Check that the riders know their numbers.

- Turn the ride down the centre line in single file.

- Before number 1 reaches the end of the school, instruct each rider to go right or left at the end. (Young children will be unlikely to understand odd and even, so call out their actual number and make sure they know which way they are to go – they could indicate by putting out their hand before the end of the school – or tell them to go the opposite way to the rider in front.)

- The riders should be double distance apart and not close up.

- Try to get them to keep level with their opposite rider.

- They must pass left hand to left hand but far enough apart that they cannot touch each other.

- Turn down the centre line in pairs.

- First pair to the right (specify who that is), second pair to the left, etc.

- Up the centre in fours (if numbers allow).

- You can either divide up in pairs again at the end of the school, or, if room, turn one four to the right and the next four to the left.

- Up the centre as an eight and halt.

- You can then show the ride how to salute.

- Reverse the process then to get the ride back to single file.

(You will all then need a rest!)

Teaching points

- Do not try this with any ponies whose temperament (especially where kicking is concerned) you have doubts about.

- When riding in pairs, threes or fours, make sure each rider gives his partner(s) plenty of room, and that the one nearest the school fence does not get squeezed.

- Make sure the children fully understand what they are going to do.

- Ensure they know what left hand to left hand means.

- Make it fun, and give plenty of praise and encouragement.

- Once children have mastered the idea of the drill procedure, you can introduce scissors across the diagonal.

- One of the most popular activities is turning a drill ride into a musical ride. Children adore doing this; it makes a very suitable display for parents and is enjoyed by all.

CIRCLES

LEARNING TO RIDE A CIRCLE

- Place a cone in the centre of the circle to be ridden. Tell the riders to pretend they are on a piece of string, one end attached to the cone, and the other to their hand. See how evenly they can keep the distance from the central cone as they ride round on a circle. It is

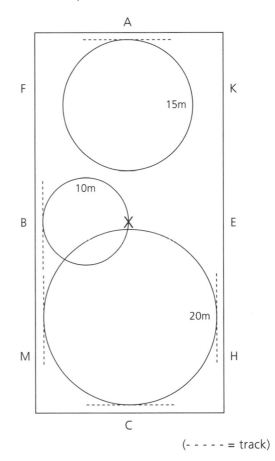

(- - - - - = track)

Three different-sized circles: a 15m circle starting at A, a 10m circle starting at B, and a 20m circle starting at C. The rider should begin to leave the track when his leg is level with these letters.

important that the children look round the circle they are riding. As always, 'eyes first'. You can then move the cone to another site and see if the children can ride a good, even-shaped circle around it.

Eyes first!

- Explain that all school circles start at an arena letter. You can demonstrate the shape of the circle by walking it yourself. In fact, you can play 'Follow my Leader', with you as leading file, practising riding circles. Call out the name of the letter and the size of the circle as you start the circle.

- If you have a quiet pony, you can try exercise (a) using a real piece of string or rope – children really enjoy this. This can only be done if you only have just a handful of riders, otherwise the other children quickly become bored or cold while waiting for their turn. Give the child one end of the rope, ensuring first that there is no loop at the end, and that the child holds the end flat: on no account should they loop it or wrap it round their hand. Then stand in the middle of the circle and hold the other end of the rope yourself, and ask the rider to walk round you on the circle. Make sure the child knows to let go if in trouble. Walk initially, and only trot if the child is reasonably capable and co-ordinated enough to be able to let go if need be.

- In a sand school, draw a circle in school surface, which the riders must follow. Make sure each rider stays on the correct track.

- Place cones or poles on four points of a circle (the tangents) and encourage the children to ride from one point to another, rounding off the sides to form a circle.

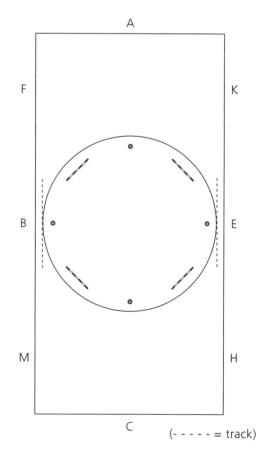

(- - - - - = track)

Poles and cones used to help ride a correctly shaped 20m circle at E/B.

PRACTISING CONTROL

CIRCLING TO THE REAR OF THE RIDE

About this exercise

- The leading file circles to the rear of the ride. As each rider takes a turn at being leading file, control is improved.

- Makes the children aware of pace and timing.

- May be executed in walk or trot.

Teaching points

- Make sure the leading file rides a good shape and times their arrival at the rear of the ride correctly.

- The rider must look where he is going as he turns.

- Keep an eye on the next leading file, who must not allow his pony to follow.

- Strong encouragement may be needed to make the child keep his pony going.

CIRCLING TO TAKE LEADING FILE

About this exercise

- Here the above exercise is reversed and is more difficult because, on the whole, ponies are reluctant to take the lead.

- This may be executed in walk or trot.

Teaching points

- Be careful that the pony does not try to cut in too soon and then try to kick the existing leading file. For this reason, the child needs to aim quite some way ahead of the leading file.

- Both these exercises can be varied, by choosing a child at random, and instructing him to either circle to the rear, or take the lead. This keeps the children attentive and makes them listen to instructions.

- You can also incorporate 'Simon Says' into the instructions.

- Children enjoy any element of surprise.

COMPETITIVE EXERCISES

Children love to be competitive, so anything involving some good-natured rivalry is 'in' with them. Sometimes it is not easy to find games that cater for a wide variance in the ponies and children. One game that makes provision for the slow, lazy pony yet challenges the forward-going, active pony is 'Who can make their pony go the slowest without stopping?' This gives everyone a chance to be good at something. Never allow a child to feel inadequate, and certainly never indicate that the pony is anything other than very special (even if it is being a little less than perfect!)

There are endless ways of turning activities into competitions to maintain enthusiasm and interest. There is nothing like the sharp edge of competition to keep everyone alert! However, not every child is highly competitive and you must be aware if anyone is not enjoying the games. It may be that they will need more encouragement and a different game that allows them to shine. (You can always cheat a little in the judging so that everyone has a turn at winning!)

Here are a few ideas for competitive games where the riders learn through play:

'Who can stand up in the stirrups first?'

'Who can sit down first, without thumping down on the saddle.'

'Who can put their hand on their pony's ... mane?' (There are numerous parts of the pony, tack and the rider's body that can be used to make this great fun.)

'Who can make their pony walk in the straightest line?' (Up the centre, across the diagonal, from E to B, just off the track, etc.)

'Who can stop their pony without me seeing their aids?'

7 TROTTING

If trotting is to be included in the lesson, it is a good idea to do it while the children are fresh. Trotting is hard work for little children, so it is vital not to persist if they are tired.

Children need to learn how to master the rising trot. Some ponies are easier to learn on than others, and the very short-striding Shetland is probably the most difficult. Some children pick it up quicker than others, but eventually all children will succeed – in much the same way as they suddenly find their balance when learning to ride a bicycle.

Most children, before they know how to do the rising trot, dislike the sensation of bouncing up and down on the saddle. Little boys find it particularly uncomfortable.

- Trot on the straight only. Going round corners places too much emphasis on the child's balance while he is trying to master a new skill.

- It will depend on the child whether he needs to hold the neck-strap with one hand or both.

- Before you do any trotting, check that everyone has trotted before.

- Find out who can or cannot do the rising trot.

- Check that they know to hold the neck-strap when they trot.

- Always trot one at a time initially, even with children you know. Ponies are unpredictable, and if one is fresh it can cause havoc with a ride and upset the children.

- Only trot singly or in twos if you have beginners in the ride. Trotting en masse can cause excitement even among the most placid ponies.

- Depending on the size of the arena, the ability of the child, and the fitness of the runner, decide how far each rider should trot. For example, ask them to trot from one letter to another (another way of practising learning letters).

- Watch each child carefully, making sure he is managing, and be ready to remind the leader to hold the child's leg if need be.

INTRODUCING A CHILD TO TROTTING

- Have an experienced leader.

- Explain to the child how it will feel when the

pony trots.

- Make sure the child is holding either the handle on the saddle, if there is one, or the neck-strap.

- Hold the child's lower leg.

- Ask the pony to take just a few slow, but even, trot steps.

- Encourage the child and praise him.

- Repeat.

- Allow the child to get used to the sensation.

TO INTRODUCE RISING TROT

The sooner a child masters rising trot, the better, because the bumpy action of the trot is extremely uncomfortable initially.

- Have an experienced leader.

- At halt, encourage the child to stand up in the stirrups and sit down again (gently) At first, the child will only be able to do this very slowly, but gradually the speed of rising can be speeded up by you counting one, two, one, two. Without the action of the trot to help, this is very tiring,

The rider is using his neck-strap to help keep the balance in the rising trot. He is looking where he is going and has a soft contact on the pony's mouth.

especially for a child. Try the same in walk before progressing to a few strides of trot. Accept that it will be a case of the child literally going up and down, and not doing a proper rising trot movement.

- Encourage the child to grow tall and lean forward slightly as he uses his legs to ask the pony to trot. It helps the child with the unexpected forward motion if he, too, is asking the pony to trot as well as the leader.

- The leader should have hold of the child's leg for the first few times into trot until the child seems secure.

- If a child loses his balance, he will then become tense, which will make it all the more difficult to keep balanced.

- It is the transition from pace to pace which is the most unbalancing moment for a rider, so be prepared for the transition back to walk by making sure the leader is holding the child's leg.

- Make sure the transition back to walk is well before any turn or corner to avoid loss of balance.

- Make sure the pony trots in an even rhythm and not fast.

- Do not trot for too long.

Faults

These include rising too high, staying up too long, missing several beats, clutching the reins for support, pushing off the toes, losing the stirrups, wobbling about or being left behind. Encourage the child to lean forward and go back to standing up in the stirrups. Then get the child to try again by saying to him up, down, up, down.

NEXT STAGE IN MASTERING RISING TROT

- Make the child go up and down in the saddle at walk, saying 'up, down' at the same time.

- Proceed into trot as before, with the child standing in the stirrups.

- Then encourage the child to sit and stand again, saying 'up, down' at the appropriate moments.

- A good concept is to tell the child to imagine there is a drawing pin on the saddle and that every time he sits, it will hurt, so he must say, 'Ouch!' This helps the child grasp the idea of rising up again quickly, and the word 'ouch', being said in time with the trot, helps the child feel the rhythm. The child will eventually feel the movement in his own time.

- Teach the timing of the trot by saying, 'One, two; one, two' in rhythm.

- The leader must be prepared to hold the child's lower leg if the child wobbles.

PRACTISING THE RISING TROT

Eventually the child will pick up the rhythm of the trot. The more regular and rhythmical the pony's trot, the quicker the child will master the technique.

Remember: children will find this very tiring, so do not work at this for too long. You can introduce short trots throughout the lesson to practise. In time, the child will learn how to rise without any problem. Do not try to make it happen too quickly – the child will learn in his own time.

A competent child who has found the balance in trot can be asked to trot for short periods without holding the reins, with his arms cupped (not folded, because they can be released much quicker in an emergency). This helps further improve balance and security and develops a more independent seat.

SITTING TROT

Once a child has mastered rising trot and can keep the rhythm on turns and circles, he can try a few strides of sitting trot.

The easiest way of introducing sitting trot is to instruct the child to make a transition from walk to trot, but he is not to do rising trot until you tell him. Allow him to do several strides of sitting before telling him to rise.

Initially, the child will lose balance, he will bounce about and his hands will bob about, probably jerking on the reins. To rectify this,

encourage him to relax as much as he can to feel the movement of the pony underneath him and keep his hands down. He will be pulled forward if he tries to hold the neck-strap, but he could hold the pommel of the saddle with one hand and his reins in the other.

- You may need to hold the child's leg , or employ a leader to do so, especially on a corner, to steady the rider.

- Often the weight will come out of the stirrup and as a result, stirrups may be lost.

- Encourage the child to sit up straighter than when he does rising trot.

- Only do this for short periods because it is tiring for the child and uncomfortable for the pony.

- Gradually increase the periods of sitting trot by getting the ride to sit on the short sides of the school and rise on the long side.

- As balance improves, so will the ability to absorb the movement of the sitting trot.

TROTTING EXERCISES

Depending on the ability of the ride, many of the turns, changes of direction and transitions can be executed in trot.

- **Trotting one at a time to the rear of the ride** while the rest of the ride remains in **walk**. This improves control not only for the one trotting, but also for the new leading file.

It gives everybody a chance to be leading file for a while.

- **Trotting one at a time to the rear** of the ride, incorporating a **circle** round you somewhere on the way. This gives the child the feeling of riding on his own instead of perpetually following another pony. It makes the child ride positively in trot, and you can encourage enthusiastically as he trots around you.

- **Circling to the rear of the ride** (to be avoided with ponies who are only too happy to cut back to the ride, because this exercise rather encourages this!)

- **Taking the lead from the rear**. Make sure the child does not cut across the leading file or ride too close to the other ponies.

- **Standing up in the stirrups** to practise balance – make sure they hold their neck-straps.

- **Forward swing** as practice for jumping position – make sure they look through their ponies' ears and keep their heels down.

- A fun game is to ask each child, as he does rising trot to the rear of the ride, to **make an animal noise every time he sits**. This causes great hilarity (the shy child soon becomes bolder!) and yet, at the same time, the child is learning to keep the rhythm.

- **Singing** is another way of improving rhythm. Making the ride sing a suitable marching song as they trot round the school not only helps maintain rhythm and pace, but also relaxes

the children (it can also be a good way of letting off steam for a boisterous ride!).

By taking their minds off the actual riding of their ponies, balance, security and position can all be improved, often with very little effort from the children.

- **Riding to music** – old favourites like the 'Grand old Duke of York' are great fun for children to ride to. They can stand up in their stirrups on the words, 'When they were up, they were up...' And sit to, 'When they were down, they were down...'

By **pretending to be soldiers**, the children, through play-acting, will develop good posture.

Music helps develop a feeling of rhythm as well as adding to the fun of a lesson.

Any marching type music is ideal.

WORKING WITHOUT STIRRUPS

- Improves balance and security by dropping the seat down into the saddle.

- It is hard work and should be done for short periods only.

- This should only be attempted by children

who have gained reasonable security in the saddle with stirrups.

- It is best to cross the stirrups in front of the saddle, making sure that the child is comfortable. Pulling the buckles down on the leathers prior to crossing them makes the skirt of the saddle less bulky and less likely to hurt the child's thighs.

- Trot for short periods only, on the straight – a child is likely to slip to the outside on a corner and unless he corrects this by putting more weight on the inside heel, may easily slide off altogether.

- It is a good idea to have a leader running beside the pony initially who can hold the child's leg if necessary.

- The reins should be knotted, and the child should hold these in the outside hand and hold the pommel of the saddle with the inside hand.

- When a child has mastered sitting trot without stirrups, he can try to do a few steps of rising trot without stirrups. This is very strenuous and should only be done for very short periods of time.

8 USING POLES IN LESSONS

Work with poles can be used to great advantage, in numerous ways, with riders of all standards. By using just a few poles, you can brighten up a lesson quite considerably.

- Poles help to keep the children's attention.

- For the young child they are invaluable in creating different problems and challenges.

- By using poles to create all sorts of imaginary scenery for playing games you can have a great deal of fun, but still be teaching. Children, with their vivid imagination, love to play 'pretend games', which in turn help improve control, balance and confidence.

- Poles are useful in teaching children to ride correct circles (see page 72) and shapes.

- They can be used (see page 85) to help children ride correct corners.

- Poles can prepare children for jumping.

When working a pony on its own, always line up the rest of the ride in the middle of the school. Most ponies will invariably come back to the ride if the rider lose control for any reason, and this helps avoid a pony galloping off towards the gate and home.

GAMES USING POLES

HALTING OVER POLES

- An excellent exercise to help improve control of the pony.

- Scatter poles randomly around the school.

- Send the ride off round the school at walk. On command, the children must ride to the nearest pole and ask their pony to halt, straddling the pole.

Teaching points
- Make sure the children present their ponies straight at their chosen pole.

- You can award good marks as appropriate.

- You can vary the game by appointing a particular pole to each child.

BENDING THROUGH POLES

- Place several poles approximately 3 metres (10ft) apart.

- Ask the ride to weave in and out of poles.

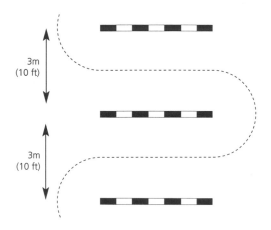

Poles used for bending.

- Can be done singly, or, using two sets of poles, can be made into a relay game.

- Children learn hand and leg co-ordination.

- Teaches balance and gentleness as they use the aids.

- Make sure the children look where they are going and use their body, not by leaning, but by turning the way they want their pony to go.

STARTING STALLS

- Use poles as 'starting stalls' on the centre line.

- Useful aid for lining up the ride in an orderly fashion.

- Presents a challenge for the children to steer

their pony into the requisite stall each time they line up.

- You can ask the ride to walk through the stall, or ask them to halt there.

- Using two sets of starting stalls in line with each other the ride can walk through both, keeping a straight line in between. This is good practice for steering and keeping the pony straight.

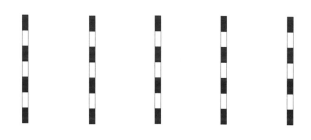

Five poles used as starting stalls for four ponies, or for lining up the ride in an orderly manner.

CROSS-ROADS GAME

- This is always popular and great fun even with the slightly older child.

- Place poles to form a cross-roads in the centre of the school.

- Ensure that the 'roads' are wide enough to avoid any kicking.

- Divide the ride into, say, juggernauts and sports cars.

- Explain which road has right of way.

- Explain that the sports cars must give way to the juggernauts, unless they can accelerate (trot) to get out of the way.

- Make the children ride up to the road junction. Stop. Look right then left, then right again before deciding whether they can cross. If there is any 'traffic' coming, then they must wait until the 'road is clear'.

- Change over the juggernauts and sports cars.

- You can vary the game by allowing the riders to turn right or left when they arrive at the junction. Make them put out their arm to show which way they intend to go.

- Remind them which side of the road they must 'drive'.

- This is good practice for road safety as well as control of the pony and general awareness.

MAZES, TRACKS AND TRAINS

- Poles on the ground can create mazes, tunnels, roads, railway tracks, trails, etc. (see diagram). You can build a station with ponies as engines, carriages, guards vans and have you as the stationmaster, blowing a whistle. (Take note that matters tend to get rather noisy if you entrust a child with the whistle!)

- Give every rider a chance to be the engine.

- A great game for improving control and balance as well as providing huge entertainment and enjoyment.

- With imagination and enthusiasm, you can keep a ride amused for ages!

Poles used to create a maze for steering practice. Many different patterns can be created depending on the number of poles available.

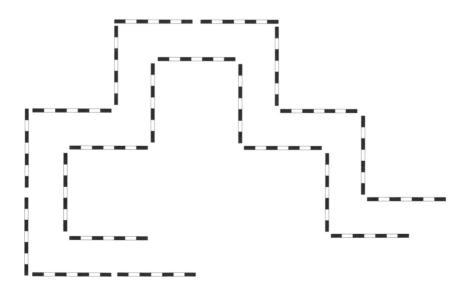

WHO CAN RIDE THEIR PONY THE STRAIGHTEST?

- Using two poles on the centre line, which you gradually roll closer together, you can see who can steer their pony between them without letting the pony run out.

- This is a good exercise in learning that the rider must use the leg to keep the pony straight (rather like pedalling a bicycle to prevent it wobbling) as well as keeping an even contact on the rein.

- This teaches the children to look where they are going as they turn up the centre line, and to keep their ponies straight once they have turned.

Rider looking straight ahead to help keep pony on a straight line.

SLALOM

- Poles can create 'gates' which the children have to steer their ponies though.

- Can be done singly or as 'Follow my leader'.

- If room, two courses can be built, so allowing for a relay race.

- This is good practice for control and balance and by making it competitive, you will increase the determination of the riders to make their ponies go where they want them to go.

Poles used to build a 'slalom', with cones used as the start and finish and for turning round before coming back.

USING POLES TO AID RIDING SHAPES

SERPENTINES

By the strategic placing of poles and cones, children can learn the shape of a serpentine.

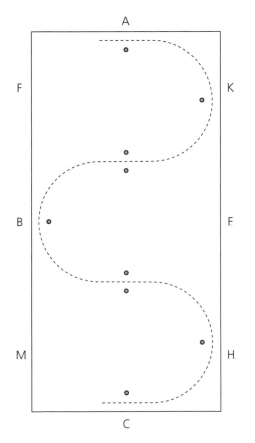

Cones used to help ride a correctly shaped serpentine.

RIDING CORNERS AND CIRCLES USING POLES (See also page 72)

When children come to jump, it will be so much easier for them if they have learnt how to ride round corners correctly. Even at an early age, they should appreciate that they should try to keep the same speed and regularity, i.e. learning rhythm from the outset. You can use the word 'balance' even though they will not

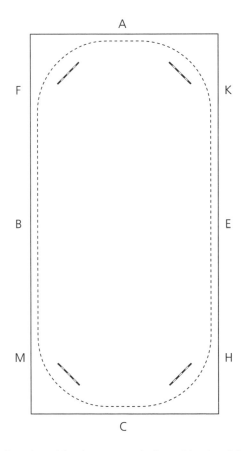

Poles placed in the corners help guide the riders round the school. The poles must not be put too deep into the corners because this makes the corners too sharp, which may cause the children to lose balance, particularly in canter.

completely understand all that it implies. They will enjoy learning the words rhythm and balance, which can be bandied out throughout their equestrian life!

• Poles laid diagonally at each corner (see page 85) help children ride their corners correctly because they have to use the aids to make the pony go into and round the corner.

• Make sure that the children understand that they must guide the pony with their hand and use their legs to push their ponies round the corners, using the inside leg to prevent the pony from cutting in.

CHANGING THE REIN AND UP THE CENTRE

Emphasise that the pony must be straight after turning across onto the diagonal.

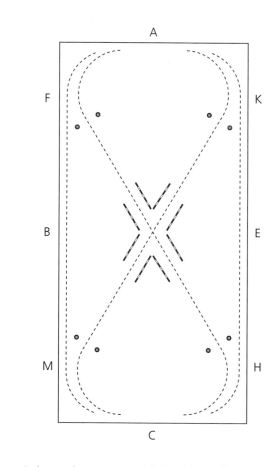

Poles and cones can help to teach how to ride a correct turn up the centre and to encourage riders to keep straight on the centre line.

Poles and cones can aid the riding of accurate turns across the diagonal to change the rein.

RIDING OVER POLES

Children should look forward to riding over poles and eventually jumping.

At all times, confidence must be nurtured, and a child should never be forced to do something that he is genuinely frightened of doing.

As with trotting, any work over poles or jumps should be done while the children are still fresh (but not the ponies!).

- Place one pole alongside the side of the school or hedge to help keep the pony straight.

- Make sure the children are holding their neck-straps.

- The ride should then firstly walk over a single pole.

- Make sure there is at least one pony's distance between riders.

- It is easier to start with a follow-my-leader situation, rather than one at a time, but you can move on to working individually once the children are confident and, in the case of those off the leading rein, the ponies sufficiently obedient.

- If you are uncertain about any of the ponies and you suspect they may jump the pole, rather than just step over it, make sure you have an experienced leader who can hold the child's leg.

- Walk over the pole from both directions.

- Make sure the children look where they are going when riding over the pole. Children have a habit of looking down!

- When you are happy with the way the ponies and children are coping with the one pole, the ride can then trot over it, one at a time, being led as necessary.

- A second pole and then further poles (depending on the standard of the ride) may be introduced, but place them 2.5m (or approximately 8 ft) apart to allow for two trotting strides.

- Do not place two poles at a trotting stride at 1.25m (or approx. 4 ft) apart because the ponies might try to jump the two poles, which could easily frighten the riders.

- You can then place the poles away from the side of the school fence so that the children have to keep their ponies straight without the help of the school as a wing on one side.

EXERCISES OVER POLES

FOLLOW MY LEADER

Scatter poles around the school and play 'Follow My Leader'. Choose a reliable leading file who can make sensible turns into each pole. Make sure the children look where they are going, ride over the middle of each pole, and maintain an even pace, so keeping an even distance from the pony in front. This is good fun for the ride as well as teaching about turns and lines into fences.

PRECISION RIDING

Tuck a hanky or a leaf round the middle of a pole and see if the children can steer their ponies over it. Move the hanky or leaf off-centre and see if they can still make the ponies go over it without running out. This is a good lesson in learning how to use the leg in conjunction with the hand to keep the pony straight.

RIDING OVER POLES IN PAIRS

Choose your pair carefully to avoid any chance of kicking. The children enjoy this and, as an exercise, it helps to improve control.

FORWARD POSITION

Explain forward position. Then practise walking over poles in forward position.

ABOVE: Forward position. The rider has a light contact with the pony's mouth. He is looking up and his heels are down even if the stirrup has slipped 'home' This is a more secure position for the stirrup for jumping, hacking and cross country riding until the child has a stronger lower leg.

The rider is looking up, his balance is good and he has a soft contact on the pony's mouth. The pony looks happy and confident. as does the rider.

STANDING IN STIRRUPS

Practise trotting over a single pole or line of poles with the children adopting forward position as they come to the poles. They need to bend at the waist and keep their legs 'glued' to their ponies sides.

Make sure they hold their neck-straps, look ahead and keep their heels down. This is good for the balance and prepares the children for jumping later on.

Children should learn this position from an early age. You are aiming for minimum movement of the child over poles and later over an actual fence. (See drawing on page 88.)

DIRECTION GAME

A pole is placed on the centre line before X. Another pole is placed on the centre line beyond X and two further poles are placed on the diagonal from X to H and M. You stand on the centre line at C. The ride turns up the centre line and approaches the first pole looking at you. If you put out your right arm, they must go over the right pole. If you put out your left arm, they must go over the left pole. If you move out of the way, they must go straight.

This is another exercise to drum in that they must look where they are going, even if they are going over poles, and later on when they are more competent, if jumping fences.

LOOKING UP

Stand at the end of a line of poles and either wiggle your fingers or hold up fingers to count, encouraging the children to look at them. This helps them look up and ahead.

LOOKING AHEAD FOR A TURN SIGNAL

Stand at the end of a line of poles placed on the centre line and hold your hand out to indicate which way the ride should turn.

The instructor is holding up five fingers for the rider to count as he trots over a line of poles.

LINES INTO FENCES

Use poles on the ground to guide the ponies on a straight line into the trotting poles. Cones and bollards can be put to good use too, to encourage the children to make correct turns into the poles.

TURNS INTO POLES

Poles can be placed on the ground to guide the riders onto the correct line to a fence (see page 97). The poles emphasise how the pony must be straight on the approach to poles on the ground or fences.

RIDING A COURSE

Build a 'course' of poles. You can use cones to help the children with the turns into each 'fence'.

Mastering turns is invaluable for future lessons when jumping a course of actual fences. Once children understand the need to arrive straight and in the middle of each fence, jumping will be relatively straightforward for them.

You can even have a little 'jumping' competition. Line up the ponies and dismount the ride. While someone holds the ponies, you can 'walk the course' with the children to show where they must go, and the lines they must ride to each 'fence'. Point out that their ponies might be reluctant to leave the other ponies in the ride, so they will have to use their legs strongly to keep the pony going.

Finish the round with the rider halting the pony in front of you, which is all good practice.

You can judge the riders on style, which gives you leeway to be generous to the 'underdog', i.e. the most novice rider or the one with the least genuine pony.

NO STIRRUPS

Walking over poles with no stirrups helps the children feel the extra movement of the pony underneath them as he steps over the poles. Make sure the ponies are quiet and reliable.

THE MINUTE GAME

Scatter poles randomly around the school.

The children must walk their ponies over them either as a ride or individually to get them used to the poles.

They must go over the middle of each pole, they must be straight, look where they are going and plan ahead.

Then, individually, each rider has to try to negotiate as many poles as he can in a minute.

The instructor and the rest of the ride are judges, counting the number of poles, but discounting any not crossed in the middle or straight.

The children can decide, according to their ability, what speed they choose. To add to the fun you can use a 'pinger' that rings when the minute is over.

All children love this game. It involves the entire ride and not just the one in the action. It encourages forward thinking and forward riding.

It makes the children look where they are going and the ponies have to go off on their own. It is a game that cannot scare the children and it also caters for a wide range of standards.

9 CANTERING

Often a child's first canter will occur unprompted. Gymkhana games are sometimes the best way to get a child cantering without really realising what is happening. Certainly both my boys had their first canters in the excitement of trying to get their leaders to run to the finishing line as quickly as possible!

INTRODUCING CANTER

Once a child is secure, happy and confident in trot, has mastered both rising and standing in the stirrups in jumping position without losing balance, the time has come to attempt a few strides of canter.

Do not expect a child to be able to sit to the canter initially. It may well take a long time before the balance and security enable the child to sit. Try to encourage a reasonable position with the weight on the stirrup with the child looking ahead, with sufficient control of the pony.

- The child must have a leader who can not only run fast enough to allow the pony to canter smoothly, but also can hold on to the child's leg at the same time.

- As with anything new, always choose a moment when the child is warmed up but not tired and the pony settled.

- With an unknown ride, ask the children if they have cantered before.

- With any children who have not cantered before, explain how it will feel when the pony canters and show them what they must do.

- 'Hold onto the neck-strap, look up, heels down and take forward position.'

- With the rest of the ride in walk, ask the leading file to trot on and join the rear of the ride and canter a few steps on the way.

- Never canter more than one at a time.

The pony should be encouraged to canter, by you saying 'Canter' on the straight before he catches up the rest of the ride. It is unbalancing for a child if the pony canters in the corner. Always keep straight until the child gains balance and security in the canter. It is unimportant which leg the pony strikes off on.

Make sure the child is balanced and has hold of the neck-strap before the pony is asked to canter and be prepared to tell the leader to take hold of the child's leg immediately if the child loses balance.

As with transitions from walk to trot and back to walk, it is the transition that is most unbalancing for the child, therefore special attention needs to be paid to the child's security, not only when the pony goes into canter, but when he comes back to trot. The leader must be ready to hold the child's leg especially at these moments, and the canter and the transitions must be done on the straight not on a corner.

Safety and confidence first, at all times. Be patient and do not hurry progress.

Gradually, a child will become more secure and confident in the canter. This confidence must be nurtured at all times and the child's safety must never be compromised.

Once the child is secure, the leader can continue with the pony cantering round the corners.

With a very steady, reliable pony, the child can canter without a leader. Remind the child to hold the neck-strap.

As a child becomes stronger, and the balance improves, cantering will become progressively easier.

The instructor is encouraging a young rider to keep cantering whilst on a corner. She gives the rider confidence by 'cantering' upsides. The rider's hands have risen upwards due to a loss of balance caused by the weight coming out of the heel.

CANTERING WITHOUT STIRRUPS

Only when a child has good balance and is well secure in sitting trot without stirrups can he attempt any cantering.

Children will be ready to canter without stirrups at different times. It also depends on the smoothness of their pony's canter.

Canter for short periods only. A child tires quickly and loses strength.

The most unseating moments are during the transitions and on corners, so it is important to remind the child to sit up, especially if he slips to one side.

10 JUMPING

GENERAL POINTS

- Jumping should always be fun.

- The key to ensure that a child remains confident and happy when jumping is never to push him or her to do something that he or she is genuinely frightened of doing.

- Encourage a child by all means, but never force.

- You cannot make children brave by bullying them into action.

- Do not hold back the keen ones just because others are timid. You invariably find that if a 'friend' jumps, it will give courage to other members of the ride.

- Never allow a timid child to feel small, inadequate or inferior. Give praise when he or she plucks up courage to perform something, however small.

- Some ponies do not give their riders a comfortable feel when jumping and this can very quickly put a child off jumping altogether. On a different pony, that child will suddenly start to gain confidence and begin to really enjoy jumping.

- Ask questions such as 'Who likes jumping?' This will give you an indication of the attitude of the members of your ride.

- Never over-face a pony or a child.

- It is far more productive to have children clamouring for bigger fences and being told 'Next time' than to make them reluctant when it comes to their turn.

- You can provide sufficient challenges for children without making the fences big.

- If following one behind the other over poles, ensure there is plenty of room between ponies so that if the leading one should have any problems, for any reason, the one behind does not cause further trouble.

GETTING STARTED

- Always start by walking over a pole on the ground.

- Proceed to trotting over a pole on the ground. Then add another pole a second pole 2.5 metres (about 8 ft) away.

- Place wings to either side of one of the poles.

- Ensure that the children are holding their neck-straps.

- Practise forward position and forward swing.

- Make sure the children keep looking up. Stand in front of the line of poles and encourage them to look at you.

- Explain how it will feel when the pony jumps.

- Ask one of the ride who has jumped previously (a confident one who enjoys jumping!) how it feels.

- Remove the second pole and build the smallest fence possible. Either place three poles as a pyramid, or make a cross pole, not by using cups on the wings, but placing the ends of the poles on the wing feet.

- A child who has never jumped before, must have a leader who can hold the child's leg as the pony jumps.

- For most children a height of 30 centimetres (1ft) is ample. Most ponies can step over this without making a big jump. It is an unexpected leap that can put off many young children. Any fright or loss of confidence must be avoided at all cost.

- Confidence in jumping takes a long time to build, but it can be destroyed in a moment, so do not hurry progress.

- You can build a 'course' of tiny fences. Make sure you jump each one individually first before stringing them together as a course. It is a good idea to walk the course with the children, explaining why you need to walk the course. You could ask them what sort of things

A secure lower leg position, a light contact on the rein, and the rider looking where she is going presents a good picture of pony and rider jumping a cross-pole.

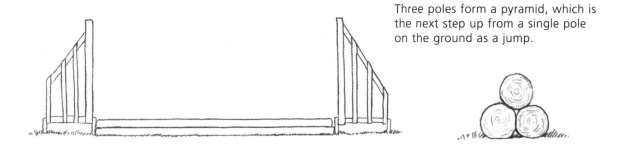

Three poles form a pyramid, which is the next step up from a single pole on the ground as a jump.

they should be looking for. Show them the correct turns into each fence (you could help with strategically placed bollards or cones) and remind them that their ponies will be less willing to go away from 'home', or the other ponies, and will need extra-strong riding to keep the same pace and rhythm. It is fun if the children run round the course, jumping the fences themselves, which not only is good practice in riding the lines to the jumps, but can warm them all up nicely on a cold day.

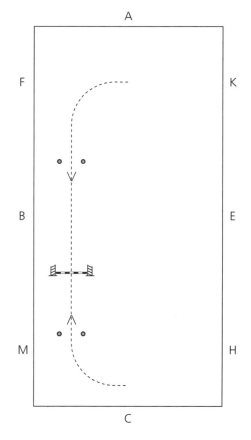

Poles and cones can be used to help guide riders onto the correct line, both into and away from a small fence.

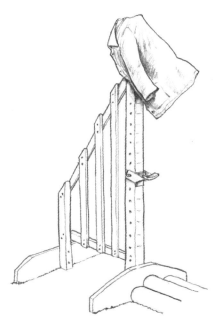

Avoid any hazards that could cause the pony to shy or injure a child if he falls off. Redundant jump cups **must always** be removed.

SIMPLE JUMPING COURSE

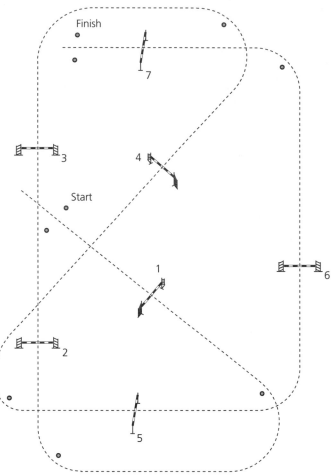

A simple 'show jumping' course with tiny fences, or even poles on the ground, and cones placed at strategic points to help the children ride correct lines round corners and into fences.

- Jumping a tiny fence as a pair, one behind the other can give a stuffy pony enthusiasm and give its rider a better feeling over a jump. Choose your pair carefully.

- Giving children tasks to do helps to relax them when jumping. You could make them recite a nursery rhyme or sing or whistle while approaching, jumping and riding away from a small jump. For  example: place one of the ride at the end of the school, and tell him to place his hand somewhere – for example, on his head, on the pony's mane, behind his back or anywhere obvious. One at a time, the rest of the ride have to jump the fence, and see if they can spot each time, where the child puts his hand. This encourages the rider to look ahead, not look down, and by taking his mind off the actual jump itself, helps the child to relax more when jumping.

- Grid work is wonderful for all age groups, once the children can jump single fences with confidence and without losing balance or the pony losing impulsion. They are therefore unsuitable for very small children.

- Once a child has become more competent, grids are excellent for developing security, confidence, communication, rhythm, balance and trust in the pony. (See Chapter 11, More Advanced Work for Older Children, on page 103.)

JUMPING FAULTS

- Common faults include getting left behind the movement, putting the toes down and losing the leg position, not folding enough, coming up too soon or not soon enough, looking down or bumping their face on the pony's neck.

- It is vital that only tiny jumps are used until the child has established a secure, balanced position. This may take months – each child will be different and not every pony is smooth and easy to jump.

JUMPING WITHOUT STIRRUPS

- The same applies as with cantering without stirrups (see page 94) but the child must be totally secure to avoid any falls.

- Keep the fences tiny and uncomplicated.

> **NOTE:** Always remove any hazards that could cause injury to a child if he falls off, such as jump cups, spare wings, broken fences, etc.

CROSS-COUNTRY JUMPING

Only once a child is confident and secure over small fences in an enclosed area can you contemplate venturing forth over different obstacles. 'Cross country' for very young children means jumping minute fences or ditches and riding up and down banks, maybe walking off a very small drop. It is crucial that a child is totally confident when asked to do anything like this. If he or she has a fright at this stage, it may damage confidence for years to come.

Remember that the ponies may react in a more energetic fashion, which means that they may well make more effort when jumping different obstacles, however small they may be. A tiny log on the ground, for example, may cause a pony to put in an unexpectedly large jump that could easily unnerve a small child.

If you have any doubt about how a pony may react to a particular obstacle, always take the child off and lead the pony over without its rider. Once you have done that a couple of times, and the pony is merely stepping over or down, you can put the rider back on and do it again with the child on board.

Ensure that the children hold their neck-straps and keep their heels down and heads up when jumping the little cross country fences you have selected for them.

Do not jump any drop fences until a child is familiar with riding downhill and is secure enough in his seat to enable him to slip his reins and sit up without holding the neck-strap. If a child keeps hold of the neck-strap when landing over a drop, he may well be pulled over the pony's head.

If, for any unforeseen reason, a child does have a fright, immediately revert to something very easy that the child enjoys, which may avoid a major loss of confidence.

Children should always view cross-country as something to look forward to and enjoy. This must start from an early age and be nurtured by their teachers.

11 MORE ADVANCED WORK FOR OLDER CHILDREN

ADVANCED FLATWORK

1. **Gait footfalls.** Introduce the ride to the various timings (beats) of walk, trot, canter and rein-back. See if the ride can hear the footfall patterns (this is not always possible on a soft surface). Explain the difference between the four-time of walk and gallop. Try to show how a pony walks by leading one very slowly. You could bandage the pony's legs with white bandages and draw on the numbers of the leg sequence.

2. **Teach diagonals.** Bandage diagonal legs and show how the legs move in pairs in trot. You can explain about sitting on a certain diagonal, but children need to be old enough to understand this concept and the reasoning behind it.

3. **Which leg?** In walk, try to get the ride to feel which leg is coming through from the hindquarters. Start with a front leg and then progress to a hind leg. Help initially but then try to see if they can feel it themselves.

4. **Monitoring pace in trot.** Get the ride to count how many times they sit between certain markers. See how consistent they can be on a straight line. Then try the same exercise on a 20 metre circle.

5. **Riding without stirrups.** In a confined space, do plenty of work without stirrups to develop confidence, balance, relaxation and security. (Not so much with boys!)

6. **Cantering circles**. Once children can happily canter from the front of the ride to the rear, you can incorporate circles into the exercise. Instruct the leading file to trot on, make a 20 metre circle at E, for example, and then ask the pony to canter on the circle before proceeding to join the rear of the ride.

7. **Transitions in canter**. Practise striking off into canter and coming back into trot at a named letter. This provides practice in control and the need for preparation in any transition. With the whole ride in walk, explain to the leading file that he or she is to trot on when he or she reaches a particular letter. He or she must then canter between the next two appropriate letters on a corner. Children should always ask their ponies to canter on a bend so you can vary the letters. For example, you could ask the child to canter between E and the centre line on a 20 metre circle from E to B or at X on a 20 metre circle at either A or C. The children will soon learn how much they must prepare their ponies to either canter or trot at a designated place. This is the beginnings of the children learning

what a **half-halt** is. Stress how the pony must keep the same rhythm as he changes from pace to pace and that this is how we know that the pony is balanced.

(A half-halt is a re-balancing of the horse or pony by the rider closing the hand briefly while ensuring the rhythm does not alter by using the leg at the same time. This has the effect of engaging the hindquarters and lightening the forehand in preparation for transitions, turns and any other school movement.)

8. **Improving the seat at canter**. Once children have confidence in cantering (and be careful not to ask any child to do anything too difficult so he loses this confidence) they can try to sit on either a leaf or a glove to help encourage them to sit to the canter and not perch forward.

9. **'On the right leg'?** See if the ride can tell if the pony is on the correct lead – 'on the right leg' – get them to watch a pony cantering and point out how the inside front leg appears to be in front of the outside one. You could bandage a foreleg to emphasise the leading leg.

> **NOTE:** Beware of asking children to see if their own pony is on the correct lead too early in their riding because it encourages the bad habit of the child looking down as the pony strikes off into canter. This bad habit can take a long time to correct.

10. **Counting the strides.** See if both the rider and the rest of the ride can count the number of strides between letters. This teaches awareness of strides and rhythm.

11. **Cantering over a pole on the ground.** You need to be cautious with this exercise because a child needs to be secure in the saddle to avoid being unseated if the pony either stands off the pole and jumps with a lurch, or takes a big jump over the pole. Always trot over the pole several times first, to get the horses and riders in jumping mode.

12. **Alternating forward position with sitting in the saddle.** This is an excellent exercise to prepare children for riding a course of show jumps or for cross-country riding. It improves balance and fitness and can be practised from quite an early age. It is alarming how few older children or adults can manage to do this with ease.

13. **Cantering with very short stirrups.** Children love to pretend they are jockeys and

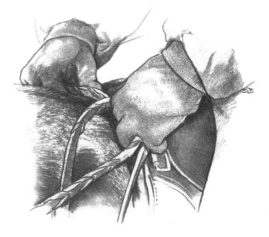

Bridging the reins.

this is excellent for improving balance and fitness. Demonstrate how to hold a bridge with the reins and explain that a bridge is useful in many ways:

(a) it helps keep the pony straight;

(b) it improves security by not allowing the hands to fall either side of the pony's neck;

(c) it provides the rider with something to lean on to help balance;

(d) it helps prevent the pony's outside shoulder swinging out on turns and corners.

MORE ADVANCED JUMPING FOR THE OLDER CHILD

This does not mean bigger fences but greater challenges. Children love challenges provided that they are within their capability. Often it will encourage them to 'attack' more and so get their ponies going forward with a more definite sense of direction.

ANGLED JUMPING

Angled jumping can only be practised once a child can hold a line to a fence. It is a fact that very few children nowadays have a chance to spend time 'playing' on their ponies and so developing a rapport or communication. It is important to get confidence early on in jumping

fences on the angle and not just straight. Initially you can use poles on the ground (see diagram). Encourage the children to keep their ponies straight and in the centre of the pole. Gradually build up to a small, straightforward fence. You can use poles on the ground to guide them.

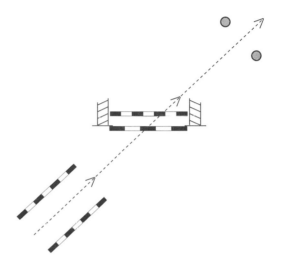

Poles and cones used to help ride correct line into fence on angle.

BLOCK ELIMINATION

Place six jumping blocks, side by side, in a line, and remove one at a time until the ponies are asked to jump over a single block. If a pony persistently runs out (i.e. more than twice) use poles to guide him in (see diagram on the next page).

This is not an exercise to use until a child is

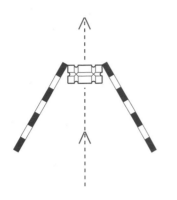

Poles used as wings into narrow fence to help prevent pony from running out.

strong enough to keep the pony straight with the leg otherwise it may give the pony the idea he can run out.

STAR FENCE

The fence can be jumped any way but the pony must be presented straight from a correct turn. This is a useful exercise to improve the speed of reaction of the rider. It practises turns into fences and keeps the rider and pony alert and prepared to jump whatever is presented.

GRIDS

You need to use extreme caution when building grids for ponies. Pony stride-lengths vary tremendously, and are affected by the forward-going nature, or not as the case may be, of the different ponies in the ride. The distances in any grid, but particularly when bounces are involved, must be correct for each pony and unless you have similar sized ponies or ones with the same length of stride, you will need to adjust the distances as necessary. **Incorrect distances can quickly damage the confidence of both pony and rider, and can be dangerous.** With a competent rider and a forward-going pony, grids are invaluable in improving jumping position, balance, confidence and security. Riders can jump down lines of little fences without stirrups, or with knotted reins, with their hands either side of the

BELOW: The star fence can be jumped from any direction, but the rider must keep the pony straight and aim for the middle of each element. The distance between elements can be 5.5–6m/18-20ft (depending on the size of pony and height of fence), which allows for one non-jumping stride.

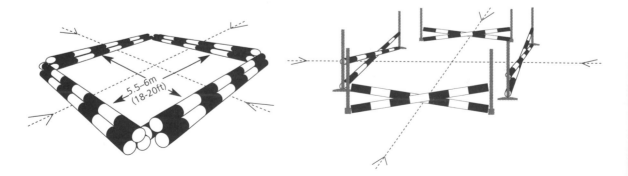

pony's neck or with their hands on their hips. This is assuming that the ponies keep a regular pace down the line and do not speed up alarmingly.

It is fun if the riders recite a nursery rhyme or sing while they jump the line of fences. This is a good way of relaxing an anxious rider, and it stops them holding their breath!

EXAMPLE OF A BASIC GRID OF TROTTING POLES WITH ONE, TWO OR THREE FENCES

1. Once the ride is negotiating the trotting poles satisfactorily, and the distances suit all the ponies, 13.2 being the average height, you can introduce a small cross-pole (which helps keep the pony straight) at approx. 2.5 metres or 8 ft

from the last of the four trotting poles. One at a time, the ride should trot over the poles, and then jump the fence.

2. Build a second fence at approx 5 metres (or 16 ft) away from the first fence. This can be a straight pole rather than a cross. The ponies should trot over the poles, jump the first fence, take one canter stride and then jump the second fence.

3. Provided that the ride is coping well with the exercise so far, you can place a third, slightly bigger, fence 5.5 metres (or 18 ft) from the second.

The above distances are approximate and you must use your judgement and experience to decide whether the distances between the fences or poles need altering. Even a small amount can make a big difference to the way a pony negotiates a line of obstacles.

A simple grid of trotting poles to cross-pole with two elements, which can be introduced gradually.

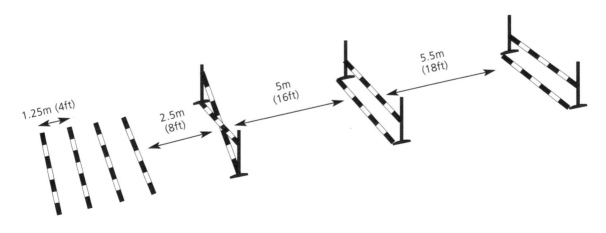

Trotting poles leading to a bounce. Remember that the distances are only approximate and may need to vary depending on the size/scope of the individual ponies and the height of the fences. For this reason, make sure the fences are **very small** initially until you have assessed the situation.

1.25m (4ft)

2.5m (8ft)

2.75–3m (9ft–9ft 9ins)

Always make sure that the fences are well presented, filled in with a sloping pole, and have ground lines.

Bounces can be introduced to the basic grid described above. Trotting poles, which help to maintain an even rhythm on the approach, are followed by a bounce at a distance of approx 2.75 metres (9 ft) apart.

When jumping bounce fences, the distances become even more important and it is imperative that they are correct for the individual ponies. Always keep the fences very small until you are satisfied that the distances are correct.

Remember: distances may need to be altered as the fences get bigger or as more bounces are added.

EXERCISE CATERING FOR RIDERS OF VARIOUS STANDARDS

- Trotting poles to fences on an angle give a ride of varying standards a challenge at all levels.

- This exercise improves concentration, confidence and control.

- Start by placing three or four trotting poles where the fences are to be built. Once the ride is trotting smoothly over the poles, you can introduce small fences.

- The children can either work individually or as a ride with each rider choosing which way he or she wishes to go over the poles and subsequently over the fences.

- The riders must keep their ponies straight on the approach to the trotting poles. They then either carry on over the second row of trotting

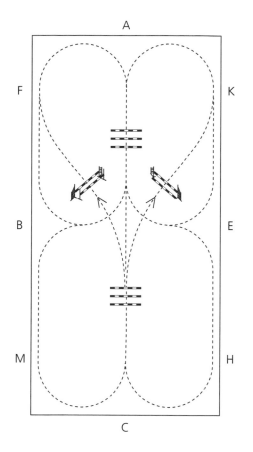

Exercise for a variety of standards. There are many different routes that the riders can choose to take depending on their ability.

poles, or turn and pop over an upright on the right rein, or a spread to the left.

• This exercise allows all the children to feel that they are participating, whatever route they choose to take. Those who do not want to jump can opt not to.

• The more capable riders, given that there is sufficient room between the poles and fences, can ask their ponies to canter after the poles on the turn to either fence.

• When working as a ride, the riders must look to see what the other riders are doing and not collide.

• The ride must pass left hand to left hand and give way by circling to allow another rider to go first.

PRINCIPLES OF JUMPING A SMALL V FENCE

With sufficient material, a fence can be constructed which allows for a corner, a bounce and a one non-jumping stride double.

Explain how you decide where to jump a corner fence by riding at the imaginary line that bisects the angle made by the two elements. Demonstrate how you need to find an object in the distance to help find a line through the fence.

12 RIDING OUT

HACKING OUT

It is important that children hack out. If they spend too long in a school they can become apprehensive about going out at all. Make sure you have a leader for each pony and keep to walking as a group until you know how the ponies react out in the open. What appears to be a very quiet pony in a confined space can have a complete character change when it spies open spaces. It is only when children are in control on very quiet ponies that you can contemplate going any faster. Even then, carefully consider how to introduce any trotting when you have a group of ponies.

Avoid traffic and always choose somewhere quiet to go for a ride. Always explain where you are going, when hacking out, so you can give precise instructions where you are in the case of an accident – and take a mobile phone with you if you can.

When hacking out, encourage the children to look about them to see what they can spot. You can teach them about animals, birds, trees, butterflies and flowers, which all adds to the interest of the ride as well as being educational.

Let the children ride in pairs because this allows them to chat, so relaxing them.

When out on a ride utilise any undulations in the terrain. Riding up and down hills teaches the children about balance. Make sure they have hold of their neck-straps, look up and keep their heels down. 'Head up, and heels down.'

If you have access to a shallow, dry ditch (having checked it is safe beforehand) practise riding up and down the banks. It can be an alarming feeling for the children until they get used to the idea of the pony going down and up again. Explain how it will feel and ensure they have a firm hold of their neck-straps, look up and keep their heels down.

Children love to ride through water. If you have access to shallow water with a safe bottom, then it will prove highly popular. Watch out for any pony that looks like rolling!

> **NOTE:** As the instructor, you must set the example on manners, so instil in your pupils that they must say thank you if someone opens a gate for them and that they wait for the person who is shutting it before riding off.

TREASURE HUNTS, PAPER CHASES AND PICNIC RIDES

You can give children a wonderful time using paper chases, treasure hunts and picnic rides. These kinds of activity need prior planning and you will need to recruit people to help set them up. Good weather is an essential ingredient for a successful time!

Taking part in these fun rides relaxes the children and gives them confidence in their ponies. As a result, they become more natural riders.

For a treasure hunt, you can use different coloured pegs or wool for different teams. Each team must follow the clues held in place by pegs or tied with wool. Always have a competent team leader as leading file.

Plan your route, and in advance, peg either a sweet or a clue, telling them which way to go, on a tree, bush or other prominent place. You can culminate with a picnic or finding some 'treasure'.

Children enjoy any sort of game where they have to be observant, and they love to be the first to spot things. You will soon have them all eagerly hunting for the next clue. With so much else to think about, nervous children tend to relax very quickly on their ponies.

Young children need this sort of fun – nowadays having real fun on ponies is something that is missing in too many of their lives. Once they get older, riding tends to become more serious, sadly, so they need to enjoy all this while they can.

13 MOUNTED GAMES

- These are an excellent way of enthusing and encouraging children to be determined and positive on their ponies.

- They provide a real means of learning through play.

- Children learn balance, co-ordination, and speed of reaction.

- Children are naturally competitive and enjoy playing all sorts of games.

- Make sure you vary the type of game so that the children and/or the ponies do not become tired.

- You can divide your ride into two teams however you choose, e.g. by colour of ponies, boys vs girls, or alphabetically.

- Avoid letting the children choose their teams themselves because you may end up with a very biased side.

- You must try and ensure that both teams enjoy their fair share of winning!

- Be careful that you maintain discipline during games time.

- You can use poles as starting stalls to keep the ponies lined up straight.

- To add interest you can use, for example, a train whistle to start each game rather than just saying 'Go!'

- You can get them to pretend to be soldiers and 'beat the drum' when they finish, on foot, whatever race they are doing (i.e. bang on a cone or plastic container).

- You can use your own imagination to create variety and added enjoyment.

- There is scope for you to improvise and make up games as you go along.

There are many different games. Here are just a few suggestions.

POTATO AND SPOON RACE

This is an old favourite that can be varied to suit your needs.

The children can either be handed a potato and spoon by a helper and then ride back holding it, or they can dismount, pick up the potato and spoon and run back. If the child drops the potato, he must stop while he replaces it before moving off again.

BENDING RACE

Use cones, barrels or poles – avoid anything that could cause injury if the pony or child bumped into it. The race can be organised in many ways. The children can ride one way, then run back (this is especially good in cold weather). You can make it a relay race, with the riders handing over a glove, a hanky, a leaf or a bean-bag at the finishing line.

LETTER-POSTING RACE

This involves riding and posting a letter. Make sure your letter-box is at a suitable height and that the ponies do not shy at either the letter or the letter-box. Make sure the leader knows which side the child wants to post the letter. In the case of children off the leading rein, have a helper ready to assist if necessary. If you have ponies who object to going near the letter-box, make the children dismount at a certain place, run and post the letter and then either remount, or run back (again, good idea if the weather is cold).

NOTE: In games where children run back to the start, the ponies must be left with leaders/helpers.

RIDE AND RUN

Or the other way round. With competent helpers to help the child mount and dismount, this is good practice for getting on and off. Make sure the ponies are facing the children as they run towards them so there is no danger of anyone getting kicked.

BALL IN THE BUCKET

Or any other improvised object. The children have to drop a ball or bean-bag into a bucket. This is good practice for aiming and control. Organise the game however you want.

BEAN-BAG/GLOVE ON THE HEAD

The children must ride and collect a bean-bag or glove, put it on their head and ride or run back without holding it. If riding back, and it falls off, the leader picks it up. When there is no leader, the child must dismount, pick up the object, remount (with help if necessary) and continue.

RUN AND FETCH

Ride up, pick a chosen object out of a bucket and run back with it.

RUN AND FIND

Ride up, pick up a leaf or some other natural object and either run or ride back with it.

'TENT PEGGING'

Using an empty detergent bottle, See if the children can pick up a bottle with a long stick. (Make sure the stick does not have a sharp end. You can use the canes from the flag race below.) Obviously you need a quiet pony for this game, and each child will need full supervision. It is best to do this one at a time, rather than make it a race.

FLAG RACE

You will need canes with flags on the end and cones for placing them in. Three canes are probably enough. The children must move the canes from one cone to another. The flags are placed in the far cone and the children must move them, one at a time, to the cone nearest them. Remind the children to ride round the cones with the flag on their inside. Good game to practise control.

HANDY PONY

You can think up all sorts of different tasks for the children to do, using a variety of props. You can incorporate some of the above games. Do not make the course too long or too difficult because the children will get tired and dispirited.

MOUNTED EXERCISE RACES

You can use round the world, half scissors, dismounting on wrong side and mounting on the near side, or vice versa (always ensuring the children run round the front of their ponies and that the ponies are sufficiently quiet and long-suffering to tolerate these kinds of games).

Every pony must be held and the holder must be ready to grab the child if he or she loses balance.

WALK AND TROT RACE

On the word 'Go', or however the game is started, the children must ride their ponies, at the walk, to a designated turner marker, then trot back. If the pony either trots during the walk, or canters when he should be trotting, he is disqualified, or given a penalty if you think it more appropriate.

With more competent riders, you can expand this game so that the children walk to a certain marker, trot to another marker, and then canter home.

Make sure that the rest of the ride is not blocking the finishing line.

'KNOCK THE MAN DOWN'

Place some empty plastic juice bottles on upturned buckets at one end of the gymkhana area. (You may need to put some water in them so they are more stable and do not blow over.) Provide each team with three or four tennis balls, which you place at a suitable distance

away from the bottles (you could even provide bottles with a face and body painted on them!).

When the whistle blows (or however you start the game), the children ride to where the tennis balls are, dismount, and hand their pony to a helper, who takes it well away from the 'firing line'. The children then throw the balls to knock over the 'man' before running back to the finishing line. (You could have the children remounting and riding to the finish, but the ponies might be frightened by the tennis balls being thrown about in various directions!)

It is useful to have a fielder who can gather up the balls for you so that you could make it into a relay race.

Children enjoy this game (they love knocking things over!) and you can make it more difficult, depending on the age of the children, by increasing the distance between the firing line and the 'man'.

All these games are tiring for young children, so do not over-do it. Know when to stop – i.e. while they are still keen and not over-tired.

CONCLUSION

In the process of writing this book, I have spoken to a number of other teachers of young children and without fail, the over-riding messages have been:

- **Make it fun.**

- **Keep the children on the move.**

- **Never frighten any child on a pony.**

- **Children must learn through play.**

- **Avoid children falling off – safety first.**

- **Be encouraging and enthusiastic.**

- **Stop before the children get tired.**

- **If you enjoy teaching, the children will enjoy being taught.**

- **Every child is different.**

- **Maintain discipline whilst keeping the lesson fun.**

In the same way that you never stop learning when riding, so you never stop learning as a teacher. By discussing methods and ideas with other people involved in teaching children, you can increase your repertoire of exercises and games and so improve your lessons.

I have always taken a notebook and pen to any lecture/demonstration I have attended and written down ideas that I think I will find useful. I also used to write down exercises and facts that I was told whenever I was taught by someone for the first time. It is amazing how quickly you can forget what you have been taught! I have drawn upon this bank of knowledge on many occasions and I often refer to my notes for inspiration. So, rather than having endless pieces of loose paper, I hope my book will be a more permanent reference for people to dip into quickly before teaching. The contents should provide them with a variety of exercises and games, as well as underlining the essence of taking a successful lesson.

INDEX

Page numbers in **bold** refer to illustrations

TEACHING NOTES

Also in this series, published by Kenilworth Press

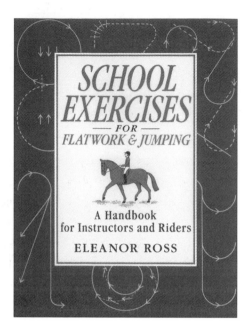

An enormously popular 'cookbook' of ideas and specimen exercises, compiled particularly for trainee instructors; also very useful for more experienced instructors and for riders schooling their own horses or ponies.

The exercises are accompanied by a full explanation, the aids, words of command, and teaching hints, and there is advice on likely problems, safety and suggested variations.

Progressive School Exercises provides a collection of exercises, on the flat and over fences, specifically designed for use in training more experienced riders and horses, whether in groups or as individuals, or schooling at home.

The book is divided into groups of related exercises, each accompanied by a full description, the relevant aids, teaching hints, and advice on remedying typical faults.

Available from good bookshops and saddlers, or direct from Kenilworth Press, Addington, Buckingham, MK18 2JR tel: 01296 715101 or visit the website: **www.kenilworthpress.co.uk** *for more information or to order on-line*